Sweet Music

by Helga Sandburg

The Wheel of Earth
Measure My Love
The Owl's Roost
Sweet Music

SWEET MUSIC

*A Book of Family Reminiscence
and Song*

By

Helga Sandburg

Preface by Carl Sandburg

Guitar Arrangements by Richard Harrison

*"A Spanish cavalier stood in his retreat,
And on his guitar played a tune, dear;
The music so sweet, would oft-times repeat
The blessing of my country and you, dear!*

—WILLIAM D. HENDRICKSON

1963

The Dial Press   *New York*

Third printing, December 1963

ACKNOWLEDGMENTS

No one owes more debts than a song gatherer and singer. But in an effort to be precise, I thank the following:

The Folklore Section of the Library of Congress, and their small and vigorous leader Rae Korson, for assistance and the use of the Archive of Folk Song.

Charlie Byrd, Washington's brilliant poet of the guitar, who was willing when his help or opinion were required.

Sophocles Papas, critic and teacher, who advised on many of the melody arrangements for this book.

Richard Harrison, who arranged the guitar chords, who uses his instrument simply and honestly, and whose grandfather never sat down to sing, but stood and roared *Hail Columbia* so country-folk heard it for miles.

Don Congdon, of the Harold Matson Company; and the patient people at The Dial Press, Richard Baron and James Silberman.

My children, as always, Karlen Paula and John Carl Steichen.

The friends and acquaintances, living and not, who have been songlovers, who wrote, composed, collected, taught, sang, listened, encouraged, and managed to be present when needed. To name a small few: Joe Glazer, Alan Lomax, Earl Robinson, Keter Betts. Others: Stewart and Lee Udall, Herblock, Ginny Byrd, Don Andres Segovia.

The scholars, in respect, politely, asking them to note that the music herein is offered in the spirit of recipes one receives from grandmothers and elderly aunts: "Lump of butter size of a walnut, egg yolk in half a shell with milk to the brim."

And lastly, in love, I thank the poet, singer, and story-teller, head of my childhood house, who sang us his songs, and who assembled *The American Songbag*, which his daughters carried about dog-eared and tattered, down to the beach, out on the dune-sides, and from room to room as they grew from girls to women.

For my elder sister,
Margaret
Who always remembers
the words

SWEET MUSIC is a sweet title and it is a sweet book.
And its author fulfills the words inscribed for her at
nine years of age in her copy of THE AMERICAN SONGBAG,
sentiments reinscribed herewith in her book SWEET MUSIC:

May you ever be nearer
to the hearts of a thrush
and a mockingbird is
the loving wish of your
everloving father: So
be it = Carl Sandburg
Connemara Farm
1 9 6 3 A D

FOREWORD

The songs that come from the people grow slowly, as they are handed from mouth to mouth, and unless there's a quality about them that the people like, they're bound to die. Almost everyone who handles a song changes it slightly to suit his taste; this is correct; it is the tradition. The songs that follow are mine. They have touched and satisfied and become a part of me. At times they differ from the way they were once sung, changing with the years.

"That is pretty," my sister Margaret said, hearing me sing one of our old songs while this book was being made, "but it's not the way we used to sing it."

I sighed, "I know. Just let me finish."

"But it's nice your way," she assured me.

"It's the way I remember."

Some of these songs I learned sprawled with my two sisters on the floor before a man and his guitar; some I picked up out in the neighborhood playing Run-Sheep-Run on a sandhill or Murder in the garage with children of the summer vacationists who came out from Chicago; some are from Michigan farm boys and girls with whom I got my early schooling; some are from farm folk who were my neighbors in south Illinois, in "Little Egypt"; some are from mountain people in the blue west hills of North Carolina; some are from modern balladiers of our day, city and country, who make up new tunes or set fresh words to old ones; and a few, to be sure, are my own.

Over the days, riding home on the bus from the Library of Congress, or pausing at my desk in the maze of papers, I have been aware that neglected was my waiting guitar. While listening to others sing, and while asking questions, and then while rambling through files and among old journals and diaries, and while leafing over dusty photograph albums, I found myself counting the time when it would all be done. I wished, in the quiet of the dark sweet city night, to take this book from a shelf and put it where it belonged, open on the stool by my chair so I could use it, guitar in my arms.

Washington, D.C.
October, 1963

Part One 1

Part Two 37

Part Three 87

Part Four 103

Part Five 133

PART ONE

. . . The years go without haste entangling their lichens,
and memory is scarcely a water-lily
that lifts between two waters
its drowned face.
The guitar is only a coffin for songs. . . .
                                        —JORGE CARRERA ANDRADE

In the dawn hours in Washington, before the sun prepares to raise itself red in the east and all the city is still, a whistler moves along the sidewalk and passes under my window. Lying in bed, listening, I am transported to other moments when I've heard other whistlers in the fresh cool of sunrises. The notes of his song are stamped on the half-dusky air.

FARE THEE WELL

One of these days, with the set - ting of the sun, The Lord's gon - na call this sin - ner home, Fare thee well, Oh my hon - ey, fare thee well!

Now and then city people will sing out, but it is done furtively, perhaps on side streets, or by the young, or some uninhibited elder. In their baths and showers they sing and whistle quite freely, and in company with others, in schools and churches. And over the country housewives in kitchens, farmers in barns, workers in factories, mills, mines. And hired hands in fields following a plow which leaves its curved pattern of flung dark earth in which the bare feet sink. And they sing in prisons and down sharecroppers' rows, the outpouring of the voices making the unbearable bearable.

In the late seventeen-hundreds, there was the vicar Thomas Percy, going through old manuscripts and finding:

> *Where gripinge grefes the hart would wounde,*
> *And dolefulle dumps the mynde oppresse,*
> *There musicke with her silver sound*
> *With spede is wont to send redresse!*

Songs are the fire of life. One is able to endure a new joy through singing. Broken hearted, one can sing the way back to a reasonable evenness of spirit. And for the ordinary chores of living, the in-between-times, songs are the seasoning for all dullness.

Back in the web of memory when I lay in my childhood bed, someone sang me a tune.

GO TO SLEEPY

Go to sleepy, little baby, go to sleepy little baby!

It was the early nineteen-twenties, and from the kitchen came songs, new ones from a new hired girl, familiar ones from a girl who'd been with us a while. We sat on her lap in a chair on the lawn, and listened to all the words.

THERE'S A LONG, LONG TRAIL A-WINDING

There's a long long trail a-winding into the land of my dreams, where the whip-poor-will is calling And the white moon beams!

I wore rompers or long blue-and-red overalls and stood on the sidelines observing, or followed my two sisters about, a hand in theirs, or on the collar of the nearby family dog. Sometimes the animal was a large black one called Charlie or Cullie perhaps. Or it was small and clownish and named Pete. Our mother liked animals and always there were kittens and dogs and rabbits at hand. The home was easy to live in; a systematized clutter surrounded her person. There were translations of German socialist tracts, books on astronomy, an old typewriter called Blickey on which she had typed our father's early poems and articles and correspondence. At one time he and she had planned their ideal home. It would be a shack in the woods with a roof, four walls, three chairs (one for company), a hat rack, a bread box, a bowl for flowers and a coffee pot. We heard about it.

But by the time I arrived, the third child, we lived in a small rented house in Maywood, a suburb of Chicago. The birth certificate listed the event: Mary Ellen Sandburg; father's occupation, Artist. Luckily he spent some time in Sweden as a reporter, during these months, and upon return, conscious of heritage, he renamed me with a Swedish one that stuck.

In the home was not only a banjo but a guitar. We called ourselves the "homey-glomies," and I listened to snatches of songs, picked them up. A repertoire of *little* songs built up; I thought they were complete and sang them the way I heard the rest sing, whether they made sense or no.

ARA-GO-ON

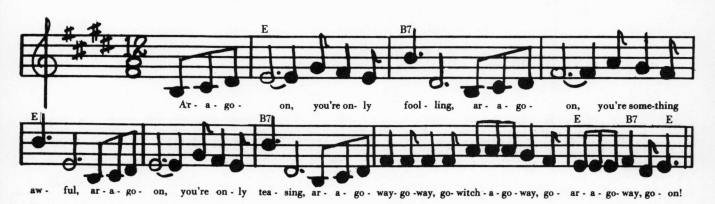

Ar-a-go-on, you're on-ly fool-ling, ar-a-go-on, you're some-thing aw-ful, ar-a-go-on, you're on-ly tea-sing, ar-a-go-way-go-way, go-witch-a-go-way, go-ar-a-go-way, go-on!

BYE, BABY, BYE-LO

Bye, ba-by, bye-lo, what makes you cry so? Bye, ba-by, bye-lo, good-bye, my lov-er, good-bye!

ELSIE

El-sie, from Chel-sea, no-bo-dy el-sie for me!

DID YOU EVER EVER EVER?

Did you ev-er ev-er ev-er in your leef life loaf' see a dee-vel di-val do-val kiss his weef wife woaf? No I nev-er nev-er nev-er in my leef life loaf saw a dee-vel di-val do-val kiss his weef wife woaf!

There was one got from our father's poet friend, a "sailorman song." Robert Frost had learned it as a boy on the wharves of San Francisco:

WHISKY JOHNNY

As we sailed on the water blue, Whis-key John-ny, a good long pull a strong one too, oh whis-key for my John-ny!

2
Whisky made me pawn my clothes, Whisky Johnny,
Whisky gave me this red nose,
Oh whisky for my Johnny!

At the head of our household was a towering vague figure who went up the stairs to a hot and dusty sunny garret. And down the stairs again, humming, singing. In the slant-ceilinged attic room large gentle hands lifted and reached me up to walk across the ceiling. In time I walked all the ceilings of the house, delighted.

A deep and slow voice told long cornfairy tales, one about the girl Blixie Bimber, one about the Potato Face Blind Man; and about the Village of Liver-and-Onions, about blue foxes, a banty hen called Shush Shush, and a girl Deep Red Roses, who loved and was left by three men: Shoulder Straps, High High Over, and Six Bits.

The tale-teller was a poet too, and in one of his books which came into the world before myself, he wrote of his songs:

Rum tiddy um, . . .
I ask you for white blossoms.
I bring a concertina after sunset under the apple trees.

I bring out "The Spanish Cavalier" and
"In The Gloaming, O My Darling."
The orchard here is near and home-like
The oats in the valley run a mile.
Between are the green and marching potato vines. . . .

As soon as I could say and remember the words, I was using the poem's songs along with the others in the house:

THE SPANISH CAVALIER

A span-ish cav-a-lier stood in his re-treat and on his gui-tar played a

tune, dear; the mu-sic so sweet would oft-times re-peat the bless-ings of my coun-try and you, dear.

CHORUS

Oh, say dar-ling say, when I'm far a-way, some-time you may think of me, dear,

bright sun-ny days will soon fade a-way, re-mem-ber what I say and be true, dear!

2

I'm off to the war, to the war I must go,
To fight for my country and you, dear;
But if I should fall, in vain I would call
The blessing of my country and you, dear!
CHORUS

3

And when the war is o'er, to you I'll return
Again to my country and you, dear,
But if I be slain, you may seek me in vain
Upon the battlefield you will find me!
CHORUS

The poem had said:

I offer you memories and people. . . .
I bring a concertina after supper under the home-like apple trees.
I make up songs about things to look at. . . .

IN THE GLOAMING

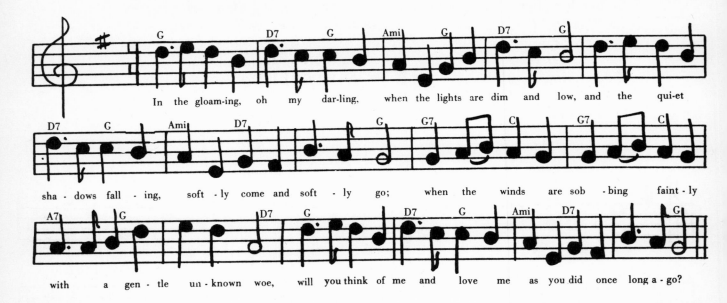

In the gloam-ing, oh my dar-ling, when the lights are dim and low, and the qui-et sha-dows fall-ing, soft-ly come and soft-ly go; when the winds are sob-bing faint-ly with a gen-tle un-known woe, will you think of me and love me as you did once long a-go?

We moved, while I was still in arms, to a country village close by. The house was once a farmhouse, parts of it near a hundred years old. There were sixty-five windows and thirty-seven doors all told. It stood along the old St. Charles Road and about it was a wood fence.

Behind was a weed-high sun-scented vacant lot where cows had once pastured. There our father worked sometimes, and a child would be sent to carry him something to eat, or coffee, or a glass of milk. He was open-shirted, his cuffs rolled up, the collar of his shirt turned under. A wood orange crate was there and papers and short pencil stubs. He had a cigar in his teeth, or else he chewed; there was the scent of tobacco on him and the scent of his sun-browning skin. Sometimes it all comes back in a daydream.

There was a kind of tenseness to him; his hair was shaggy and he was lean and he overworked himself. Tender, he had written poems for a long time to our mother. And for my sisters before I came along.

Margaret was seven years older than I; brilliant, she was reading at four. She was tolerant and gentle; she wore her brown hair in a loose single braid and pushed me in the swing, coaxed me out of my hiding place to meet company. Her father wrote:

MARGARET

Many birds and the beating of wings
Make a flinging reckless hum
In the early morning at the rocks
Above the blue pool
Where the gray shadows swim lazy.

In your blue eyes, O reckless child,
I saw today many little wild wishes,
Eager as the great morning.

In the uncut grass of the field behind our home, Margaret told me long fairy tales: *East of the Sun and West of the Moon, Old Peter's Russian Tales;* as long as I would stay she would read or tell them. We lay there for hours concealed from the world.

There was a small barn where kittens came to our cats at various times, and where dwelled the old odor of horses and hay of former days. One could play games secret and safe, in the shadow of the barn or down among the waist-tall weeds:

THE MULBERRY BUSH

We washed, wrung and ironed the imaginary clothes, swept, and scrubbed the play floors, and went to church to the tune.

Janet was two years older than I and an easy companion. We went through our growing years wearing dresses, knickers, or coveralls, cut and sewed, or purchased, in the same pattern. We clung together; she was usually persuadable and would play what I wanted to play, and we were a noisy pair. She was the beautiful one of us three, with olive-smooth complexion, dark shining hair. Her father had said:

SIXTEEN MONTHS

On the lips of the child Janet float changing dreams.
It is a thin spiral of blue smoke,
A morning campfire at a mountain lake.

On the lips of the child Janet,
Wisps of haze on ten miles of corn,
Young light blue calls to young light gold of morning.

In the house I was shy, hiding in corners. I recall the rooms as being dark, perhaps because I was always in them looking out at bright-lit scenes where others laughed and chattered. So it is in dreams. And the bureaus and beds towered; one was coaxed by a sister or adult from behind a door, tongue-tied, when company arrived. The guitar was fetched. Sometimes we got the giggles, we children.

Certain songs set us off. We spent much of our time then on the floor and under the huge round dining-room table. Growing older, one learned to stay upon chairs and sofas; for one thing you grew further from the floor. But then I hid secure, under the table, an arm about the dog who belonged to my world. Giggling I sang with the rest.

MARY HAD A WILLIAM GOAT

Ma-ry had a Wil-liam goat, Wil-liam goat, Wil-liam goat, Ma-ry had a

Wil-liam goat, it's sto-mach was lined with zinc, one- -harm in-side, but the oy-ster can!

One day it ate an oyster can, oyster can, oyster can,
One day it ate an oyster can,
And a clothesline full of shirts!

The shirts can do no harm inside, harm inside, harm inside,
The shirts can do no harm inside
But the oyster can!

At this time Leon Trotsky was writing his autobiography and in it was a passage in sympathy with us.

Then I would wink at my little sister, she would give a low giggle, and the grown-ups would look absent-mindedly at her. I would wink again, and she would try to stifle her laughter under the oilcloth and would hit her head against the table. This would infect me and sometimes my older sister too, who, with thirteen-year-old dignity, vacillated between the grown-ups and the children. If our laughter became too uncontrollable, I was obliged to slip under the table and crawl among the feet of the grown-ups, and, stepping on the cat's tail, rush out into the next room, which was the nursery. Once back in the dining-room, it all would begin over again. My fingers would grow so weak from laughing that I could not hold a glass. My head, my lips, my hands, my feet, every inch of me would be shaking with laughter. "Whatever is the matter with you?" my mother would ask. The two circles of life, the upper and the lower, would touch for a moment. The grown-ups would look at the children with a question in their eyes that was sometimes friendly but more often full of irritation. Then our laughter, taken unawares, would break out tempestuously into the open. Olya's head would go under the table again, I would throw myself on the sofa, Liza would bite her upper lip, and the chambermaid would slip out of the door.

"Go to bed!" the grown-ups would cry.

The soft poetic songs lie at the back of my memory. With them is the chink of horseshoes thrown by huge men at an iron stake. There are rearing sideboards and tables and chairs, the perfume of cigar smoke and hot coffee, and the deep voices of men talking and talking, on and on, roaring in laughter or anger. There is a banjo, or guitar strings are plucked knowingly:

STAR IN THE EAST

Star in the east, star in the west, Wish that star was in my breast, Church, I know you're gon-na miss me when I'm gone, when I'm gone, gone, gone, when I'm gone to come no more, Church, I know your gon-na miss me when I'm gone!

BYE AND BYE

Bye and bye, bye and bye, stars shin-ing, num-ber one, num-ber two, num-ber three, good Lord, bye'n bye, good Lord, bye'n bye!

In the long and endless days, life stretched ahead in an immortal unfinished pattern. I learned to use a buttonhook and fastened my own shoes. I strolled into the house and out. I heard the typewriter up in the garret which looked out over a slanted roof. Or steps moved about; he was working out poems, his Rootabaga tales, or writing for a newspaper.

"Hush," we were told, "Daddy's working."

I shrugged and carried my doll out into the yard, to go and sit in the standing wood swing across from my sister. As it creaked back and forth, I listened to *The Five Little Peppers and How They Grew* or *Quentin Durward*. She made paper doll cut-outs of the Dumas muske-

teers and clothes to fit them: swagger cloaks and tall spurred boots.
And I learned

MICHAEL ROY

In Brook-lyn Ci - ty there lived a lad and he was known to fame; his mo-ther's name was Ma - ry and his sis - ter, Ma-ry - Jane, and eve - ry Sa-tur-day morn - ing, he'd go ov-er the ri - ver, in - to the mar-ket where he sold eggs and sau - sa - ges, like - wise liv - er! For ah, for - ah, for he was me dar - ling boy, for he was the lad with the au - burn hair and his name was Mi-chael Roy!

I started school and received adjectival report cards: Conduct:
Very good; Recitations: *Very Satisfactory;* Attitude toward Schoolwork:
Very Commendable. We made elaborate notebooks, pasting colored
paper people on colored paper landscapes, and printed virtuous stories to go along:

> *This is the tree of the forest.*
> *This is the woodman who everyone knows*
> *Wielded the ax with steady blows! . . .*
> *This is the family, all are here*
> *Father and mother and children dear.*

But on the way home on South York Street, was the house of our
grandparents, Oma and Opa. I was given candy by the tall benevolent
woman, and I sinned. The sweets were to be divided among my sisters
and myself, but slowly and with increasing conviction of guilt, I finished off a piece at a time, even the last and sweetest so as to reap my
perfect harvest of sorrow. To top it off I lied to my mother.
"What gumdrops?"
I had a desire for sweets, unfulfilled. On the street outside the
grammar school, a candy wagon parked morning and night. I was
stirred by the little paper dishes of sugared butterscotch and chocolate,
the varied suckers, the colored jawbreakers. However, we were not
given candy-money. Our mother was an extremist in many ways, be-

lieved in rights of women and the laboring class, and for a while once had refused to kill a mosquito or to eat meat.

Even today I dream of the morning I entered one of the dark rooms where sewing was done, to find her great leather purse. I got a penny from it. Our hands were washed daily as we left the house, and I watched with grave panic as she unfolded the fingers and removed my coin, put it on an unreachable shelf and finished cleaning the hand. We weren't ever spanked. Both our parents were gentle presences.

Then after school, eyeing the wagon, unfulfilled, I walked home, making up new verses to a family favorite:

THE MAN WHO HAS PLENTY OF GOOD PEANUTS

The man who has plen - ty of good pea - nuts and giv - eth his neigh - bor none, shan't have an - y of my pea - nuts when his pea - nuts are gone, when his pea - nuts are gone, when his pea - nuts are gone, He shan't have an - y of my pea - nuts when his pea - nuts are gone!

2

The man who has plenty of good red ripe strawberries
And giveth his neighbor none,
Shan't have any of my good red ripe strawberries
When his good red ripe strawberries are gone!

3

The man who has plenty of sticky fresh gummy carmels
And giveth his neighbor none . . .

4

The man who has plenty of hot buttered popcorn
And giveth his neighbor none . . .

5

The man who has plenty of good corn licker
And giveth his neighbor none . . .

My sister Janet was not so aggressive as I. Sometimes she was taunted by schoolmates. I appointed myself defender, and set out each day with raised sled or slinging lunch pail. The sidewalks between home and school were regularly marked with lines on which, by some superstition, we never stepped then, and I never would in the future.

And we skirted the walks where they were ruled and numbered with colored chalk for hopscotch.

The children were lined up before the school, and we shouted, "Hasn't the door opened yet!"

In the classrooms we were taught a game and told to act it out:

FARMER IN THE DELL

The far-mer in the dell, the far-mer in the dell, Heigh-ho, the dai-ry-o, the far-mer in the dell!

And there were others. "London Bridge," and one called:

OATS PEAS BEANS AND BARLEY

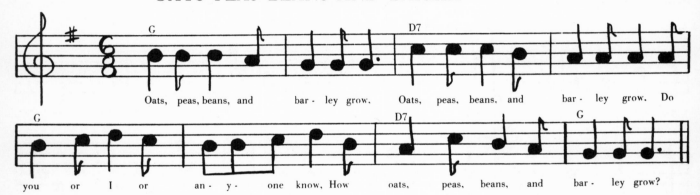

Oats, peas, beans, and bar-ley grow. Oats, peas, beans, and bar-ley grow. Do you or I or an-y-one know, How oats, peas, beans, and bar-ley grow?

2
First the farmer sows the seed,
Then he stands and takes his ease,
He stamps his foot and claps his hands,
And turns around to view the land!

At recess we wandered out to play the games that weren't teacher-supervised: jacks or jump-rope or hopscotch. The sing-song rhymes touched on illicit subjects sometimes; they were folklore and were handed down by the older child to the younger, who used them and passed them down again in his turn:

Johnny on the ocean,
Johnny on the sea,
Johnny broke a milk bottle
And blamed it all on me.
I told Ma, Ma told Pa,
Johnny got a licking, ha, ha, ha!

Red, white, and blue,
You're Dutch clean through,
Your daddy is a Dutchman
And so are you!

14

There was magic ingrained in numbers and in the alphabet letters; we used them, superstitious, to select leaders, to give prizes from first to booby, to make every decision:

Ice cream soda, lemonade punch,
Tell me the initial of my honeybunch:
A, B, C, etc.

Now you're married, you must be good,
Make your husband chop the wood;
Count your children one by one:
1, 2, 3, etc.

Skipping rope, throwing jacks, going up or down stairs.

One potato, two potatoes, three potatoes, four,
Five potatoes, six potatoes, seven potatoes, more!

1, 2, 3, 4, 5,
I caught a hen alive,
6, 7, 8, 9, 10,
I let her go again!

The First War was not long past, and swinging on swings, or sitting on the dusty cement steps in the schoolyard, with no understanding of the words we used, we sang a campaign tune for Woodrow Wilson:

WHERE DID YOU GET THAT HAT?

Where did you get that hat, where did you get that tile? Isn't it a no-bby one, and just the proper style? I'd like to have one, just the same as that, wher-ev-er I'd go they'd shout,"hel-lo! where did you get that hat?"

And the songs the doughboys had brought back with their core of bitterness to a popular tune:

2
We fought for the cause of liberty, parlez-vous,
We fought to make all nations free, parlez-vous,
But while we fought across the foam,
Freedom was killed by Congress at home,
Hinky dinky parlez-vous!

3
The YMCA went over the top, parlez-vous
The YMCA went over the top, parlez-vous,
The YMCA went over the top,
It seems they heard a nickel drop!
Hinky dinky parlez-vous!

3

The English are a peculiar race, parlez-vous,
The English are a peculiar race, parlez-vous,
They fight like the deuce until half-past three,
And then sit down for a cup of tea,
Hinky dinky parlez-vous!

Herded back to the classrooms, or to the Assembly Hall, we raised dutiful voices, affected by the brisk accompanying piano, by our just-scrubbed hands, by the control of authority. Sometimes we were so moved, we could scarce sing. It was a poem of Bobbie Burns:

FLOW GENTLY SWEET AFTON

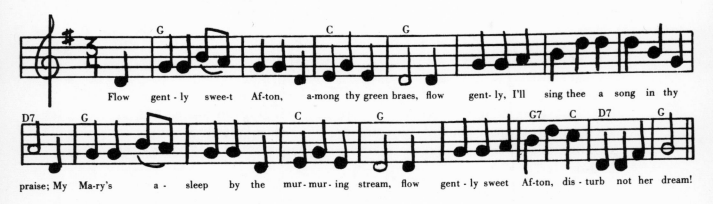

Flow gent-ly swee-t Af-ton, a-mong thy green braes, flow gent-ly, I'll sing thee a song in thy praise; My Ma-ry's a-sleep by the mur-mur-ing stream, flow gent-ly sweet Af-ton, dis-turb not her dream!

There were others; falsetto-voiced we sang them all on the way home, my eye cocked for our tormenters. Once a car halted beside us and a man leaned out, kindly.

"You kids want a ride? Get in."

"No!"

We had had instructions at home. We stood shaking our heads, awed at denying an adult. I recall the terror, and how we clutched each other's hands, used to obeying and confused by our laws.

We continued homeward, and there for comfort I crooned school songs to my dolls.

CAME A DOVE THROUGH THE WOODLAND

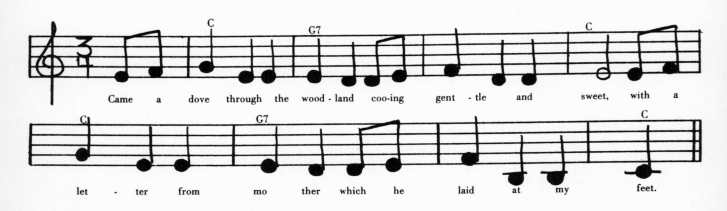

Came a dove through the wood-land coo-ing gent-tle and sweet, with a let-ter from mo-ther which he laid at my feet.

Home had a big yard and the house was white with a wood porch that rounded a corner. We had an upstairs playroom, supplied with blackboards and tables and shelves and paper and pencils. At night I heard creaking through the house's bones; it was Santa Claus or God; it was a surety that someone invisible was moving. I was confirmed in my belief that despite contrary information *someone* existed. The house must have been old to be so noisy in the dark.

In the daytime, in the side yard, there was a flower garden that comprised a small world. There flagstones wound about and somewhere at one end of a walk was a settee of wood; at the other was a hiding place where through a hedge or weeds one watched people's lower torsos and legs pass on York Street's sidewalk, whispering:

> *Everybody's got big feet*
> *Especially out on South York Street!*

Our mother moved about in the garden; it was her creation; she had an effortless manner always with green things; in and out of houses flowers turned their heads to follow her movements. The garden bordered one side of our lot. Between it and the house lay a lawn in which grew an enormous pine tree. We clambered about its bare large limbs, sat swinging our feet, singing:

YOU PUT YOUR RIGHT FOOT IN

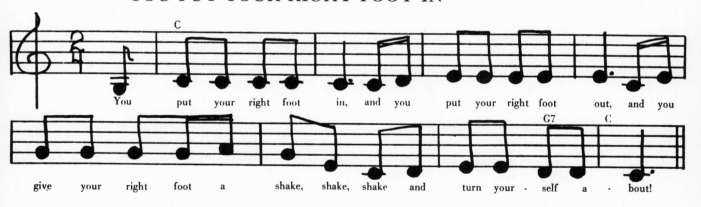

You put your right hand in and you put your whole self in. It took hours to sing.

In the garden were shaggy tall lilies and daisies and every-colored Iris and carpets of violets and small white and blue border flowers. On the walk I wheeled a low wicker doll carriage in which lay Betsy in blue corduroy round hat and coat, or some kitten persuaded into the doll's clothes. In the garden's seclusion I stayed by myself, or was followed by a dog of some kind, who came to lie near, watchful.

The dolls were necessary, alive; a part of each day was involved with them, their dressing and undressing. New ones came along now and then, more to be cared for. Sometimes an adult would take the time to make clothes and one stood by, impatient, open-mouthed, for the last button to be sewed on.

While she threaded her needle, the hired girl sang tunes she'd got from her brothers and sisters:

OH WHERE, OH WHERE HAS MY LITTLE DOG GONE

Oh where, oh where has my lit - tle dog gone? Oh where, oh where can he be? With his tail cut short and his ears cut long, oh where, oh where can he be?

It was late one afternoon and the family was in the living room. Our father was practicing catching quarters. He balanced three coins on the back of his hand, and flung them into the air, catching all three before they fell. He replaced them on his hand and looked over at me, near the door.

"She is a poker face," he said.

"Close your mouth unless you're talking," my elder sister said.

"She is the shyest of the three," said our mother. "How would you like a puppy of your own, Helga?"

"Yes," I said and came near to gaze at the faces above me.

"There are two," said my mother, "a brown-and-white and a black-and-white spotted."

"When can we go to choose?"

"Tomorrow."

"Close your mouth," said one.

"Such a poker face," said another, sighing, snatching at the descending coins he'd tossed.

"You are a prestidigitator," my mother told him, admiring, as I turned away, rushing out the door.

"No, a juggler. I would have made a good circus performer."

His voice followed me. I didn't hear. I was already planning for the coming dog. There was a fire inside now, made of anticipation, waiting to welcome another member to my family of dolls, cats, dogs. The wheels of the low wicker carriage caught on the flagstones leading through the forest of Iris. I hummed a song from the school Assembly Program. It had been composed by Julia Ward Howe as the Civil War came upon the land. She stood in her window at the

Willard Hotel in Washington, D.C., and started a poem which she set
to the tune in her ears, the soldiers singing, "Glory, glory, hallelujah!":

THE BATTLE HYMN OF
THE REPUBLIC

Mine eyes have seen the glo- ry of the com- ing of the Lord, He is tram- pling out the vin- tage where the grapes of wrath are stored; He has loosed the fate- ful light- ning of His ter- ri- ble swift sword; & His Truth is march- ing on!

CHORUS Glo- ry glo- ry hal- le - lu- jah! glo- ry, glo- ry, hal- le- lu - jah! Glo- ry, glo- ry, hal- le- lu - jah; His Truth is march- ing on!

2

In the beauty of the lilies Christ was born across the sea;
With a glory in His Bosom that transfigures you and me;
As He died to make men holy, let us die to make men free;
While God is marching on!

I sang the song of course, without understanding the words, and
if asked to write it out would render the first lines for many years:

My nice have seen the golore of the coming of the Lord,
He has trampled out the vintage where the drapes are rather stored!

Sometimes what we children said was as sensible as the original.
"Yea, though I walk through the valley of the shadow of death, I will
fear no eagle!"

It was dusk; our mother's voice was calling into the darkening
light. "Come in. Supper! Children!"

Up and down the walk I went, humming, until the call came
again, and then again. Slowly I turned to it; there was a chill coming
upon the air. I began to feel a strong need to be near others in our
house's shell. Out in the twilight was a vague threat like that of dreams.
The Iris stood stiff and stern, the drying leaves covering their feet
rustling as I shoved the tiny buggy past them. At the door I gathered
the doll into the protection of my arm and hurried in. In the event

that Betsy felt a similar fear, I held her before me on my lap while I ate, occasionally offering her something.

And after a while when the family gathered to sing, it was the same tune I had hummed while pushing the doll carriage and dreaming of the coming puppy. The song was first sung two years before the Civil War; it was set to an old slave melody. It was about a man with restless gray eyes and grizzled hair and beard, who had been just then hanged for a traitor in Charles Town, West Virginia. The world was so stirred that Victor Hugo and Thoreau, orators, poets, preachers, writers, all had argued and protested and celebrated the event. Herman Melville had shaped dark slow sentences: *Gaunt the shadow on your green, Shenandoah! The cut is on the crown (Lo, John Brown), and the stabs shall heal no more.* And John Jay Chapman said, "Everybody understands Joan of Arc and John Brown, but nobody can explain them!"

Both the North and the South used it for their war. Six hundred Negro soldiers had sung the chorus at Poison Springs, Arkansas, as they marched into the battle. And the head of our household had written about him too, in *Osawatomie:*

> *I don't know how he came,*
> *Shambling, dark, and strong.*
> *He stood in the city . . .*
> *Always he kept on asking: Where did that blood come from . . .*
> *They hauled him into jail . . .*
> *And he wrecked their jails . . .*
> *Always asking: Where did that blood come from?*
> *They laid hands on him . . .*
> *And the necktie party was a go, by God.*
> *They laid hands on him and he was a goner.*
> *They hammered him to pieces and he stood up.*
> *They buried him and he walked out of the grave, by God,*
> *Asking again: Where did that blood come from?*

JOHN BROWN'S BODY

John Brown's body lies a-mouldering in the grave;
John Brown's body lies a-mouldering in the grave;
John Brown's body lies a-mouldering in the grave;
And his soul goes marching on!

CHORUS

Glory, glory, hallelujah;
Glory, glory, hallelujah;
Glory, glory, hallelujah;
His soul is marching on!

2
He captured Harpers Ferry with his nineteen so true
And he frightened old Virginia till she trembled through and through;
They hung him for a traitor, themselves the traitor crew;
And his soul is marching on!

The stars of heaven are looking kindly down!
John Brown died that the slave might be free!
He's gone to be a soldier in the army of the Lord!

And one of the parodies that sprang up ran:

They hanged Jeff Davis on a sour apple tree,
A long time ago!

Out in the country at this time—it was the twenties—was trouble. Years had passed since the restless-eyed man had been hanged, but the tune was being put to work again. It was needed by lean worried men standing on picket lines, to bolster and warm them. We children sang, knowing nothing of hunger or striking coal miners or the Kanawha Valley in West Virginia:

SOLIDARITY FOREVER

When the union's inspiration through the workers' blood shall run;
There can be no power greater anywhere beneath the sun;
What force on earth is weaker than the feeble strength of one?
The union makes us strong!

Solidarity forever;
Solidarity forever;
Solidarity forever;
And the union makes us strong!

2
They have taken untold millions that they never toiled to earn,
But without our brain and muscle not a single wheel could turn.
We can break their haughty power, gain our freedom when we learn
That the union makes us strong!

3
In our hands is placed a power greater than their hoarded gold;
Greater than the might of armies magnified a thousandfold;
We can bring to birth a new world from the ashes of the old,
For the union makes us strong!

Before long our father said to our mother, "Now I'm going up to work, Buddy."
"One more song," we clamored.
"No," he said.
"Please, Daddy!"
"You may as well, Buddy," my mother coaxed.
And it was one he'd sung with college chums in years before:

THEN IT'S A HOO-RAW

Then it's a hoo-raw and a hoo-raw, thru the mer-ry green fields, a hoo-raw! stand-ing on the walls of Zi-on, Zi-on, see my ship come sail-ing, sail-ing, stand-ing on the walls of Zi-on, see my ship come sail-ing home!

And then he kissed us, first my sisters, with "Goodnight Spink. Goodnight Skabootch." And he gazed down on me, "And what will we call this one for short?"

Open-mouthed, I stared up. "Walk me on the ceiling now."

"Tomorrow," he promised. "And I've got to find a name for you that sticks." He was gone, climbing the stairs, humming, and in a little while the patter of the typewriter was heard, and then his feet moving on the attic floor.

"To bed, you three," our mother said.

We squealed on the steep staircase. "I'm first. No I'm first!"

My brown-and-white puppy barked. "Be quiet," I yelled, "don't you know Daddy's working!"

Our mother sighed, "If you can all tiptoe and whisper too, I'll tell you a story."

"Okay."

"Shhhhh."

"Listen."

We had warm beds, and we asked to hear of old days, family stories retold all through our lives, changing slightly in the telling so as the years passed there would be arguments. "No, it happened this way. I remember Mama said." "Nonsense. She told it the other way. I always remember right!" In the same way songs changed. "This is the way we sang it," I shook my head at my sister. "You're wrong. You are wrong, Helga."

And our mother sat beside the bed and talked. It was history, personal sometimes when she told us of ourselves, of Janet and me in rompers, pulling off the Christmas-tree ornaments one year and circling about, trampling the fragile balls to bits, while we sang carols with pagan enthusiasm.

Some of her talk was in the swing of the nation. Our parents were both children of immigrants, proud they were of plain unlettered peasant stock. In their childhood homes the languages of the old country had been spoken: Luxembourg, French, German, Swedish. And in the way of first-generation Americans, they used clear and careful English, conscious of their prose. During the turning of the century, they had read the poets and the philosophers, and they felt their part in the breaching of old laws and the making of new. The rights of women and laboring men were being worked out, and the education of the young; they saw the coming into being of the new leisure class which was to devote itself to the arts.

There was the story of the child "Charlie," our father, whose diapers had been of flour sacks and who slept on a cornhusk bed, who ate bread spread with lard and sprinkled with salt, liking it. He had got his first banjo for two and a half dollars. Once our parent had been a porter and bootblack in his town's barbershop. Our grandfather couldn't write his name. Young Carl had stepped out of his home early, to make his own way, traveling about the country in boxcars, even arrested and taken to jail, "forcibly detained," now and then.

He had always sung us jailbird songs, a jolly one:

PORTLAND COUNTY JAIL

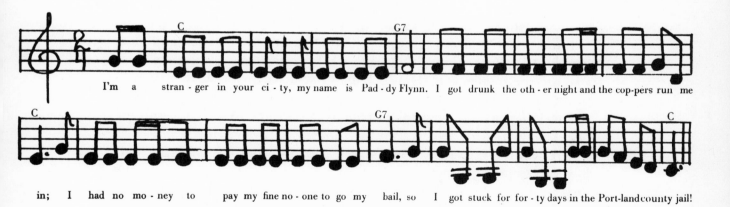

I'm a stran-ger in your ci-ty, my name is Pad-dy Flynn. I got drunk the oth-er night and the cop-pers run me in; I had no mo-ney to pay my fine no-one to go my bail, so I got stuck for for-ty days in the Port-land county jail!

2
Oh, the only friend that I had left was Happy Sailor Jack,
He told me all the lies he knew and all the safes he'd cracked;
He'd cracked them in Seattle, he'd robbed the Western Mail,
'Twould freeze the blood of an honest man in the Portland County Jail!

3
The finest friend I ever had was Officer McGurk,
He said I was a lazy bum, a no-good and a shirk;
One Saturday night when I got tight, he threw me in the can,
And now you see, he's made of me a honest workingman!

And one with a lively beat, that I thought happy until I listened to the words:

YONDER COMES THE HIGH SHERIFF

Yon - der comes the high sher - iff riding af-ter me ri-ding af - ter me, Oh, rid - ing af - ter me,

Yon - der comes the high sher - iff rid - ing af - ter me and it's Cap - tain, I don't want to go!

2
Been down to Frankfort serving out my time,
Serving out my time, oh, serving out my time;
Been down to Frankfort serving out my time,
And it's Captain, I don't want to go!

And there were the stories of the child "Lily," our mother, and her mother, Oma, our grandmother. Oma was a milliner and once dressed Lily in quickly-got-together white voile, when the bishop came to visit their village of Hancock in upper Michigan. Lily spontaneously threw her armful of flowers into the bishop's face. We heard of the jealousy of Oma's customer-friends, who thought Lily's outfit and her behavior had been carefully thought out. We loved the tale. There was the one about Oma's arrival in the country, speaking only her Luxembourg tongue, and journeying across the country to find Opa up in the coal-hill country of Michigan. She carried our eighteen-month-old uncle in arms. Our father called Oma the She-wolf because she was so brave. And he called her the Grand Duchess of Luxembourg, respectful.

There were the details of the millinery shop, and how Oma trimmed the hats, staying up until two and three in the morning, how she copied Parisian fashions from magazines, and set the styles in the village. Once she'd got a cut-rate huge shipment of artificial roses. Ignoring our grandfather Opa's despair, she fastened one on Lily's hat and two on her own, and went to church on Sunday morning. The women drifted into her shop the following week, and soon everywhere in town were roses, roses, roses.

Then there were stories of Lily's growing up, and how in the assembly sessions in the upper grades, reciting, her black curls shook and her blues eyes were on fire. It was *The Polish Boy.*

> *Whence come those shrieks, so wild and shrill*
> *That cut like blades of steel the air,*
> *Causing the shrinking heart to chill,*
> *With the sharp cadence of despair.*
> *Again they come . . . !*

And we heard of our parents' meeting and marriage, of how she refused to wear a ring; it was barbarous; she never wore jewelry. And how the young man, Mr. Sandburg, had had raven-black hair. We had looked over the photographs of the lean tanned fellow with steel-rimmed glasses and the infectious grin, who kept himself in what the two of them called "baseball trim."

Then she was a gray-eyed and serious girl, writing poetry before she met him, a peoples' organizer in the Socialist-Democrat Party in Milwaukee. The young schoolteacher took to him right away; they married a few months after they met and we knew how packing cases were used for trunks when they moved about, and as bureaus and chests when they settled down for a while, covered with crinoline by our versatile mother. We heard about our father bringing a batch of friends home one night unexpectedly, and she had no fancy fare, but fed them pancakes far into the night. We knew the lines in the poem. He called her Paula.

> *Nothing else in this song—only your face.*
> *Nothing else here—only your drinking, night-gray eyes . . .*
> *The pier runs into the lake straight as a rifle barrel.*
> *I stand on the pier and sing how I know you mornings.*

"We ate off orange crates," she recited to us.

"We know. And you would be together for a week and then Daddy was away again, up in the Wisconsin lake country."

"Green Bay, Marinette, Sheboygan Falls, Oshkosh, among the lumberjacks."

We were asleep and she went, softfooted, to bring him hot milk or coffee, feeling how lean and worn he was, bent over his papers, the stub pencil poised. Both felt a sense of destiny about him. The household felt it, and she excused any crossness or eccentricity on his part, "After all, children, he's a genius." We accepted the fact easily.

In the mornings before the day might begin, my hair had to be done. Twenty years later St. John Perse's *Éloges* was published in America, a few lines making me at once remember.

> *"When you stop doing my hair, I shall stop hating you."*
> *The child wants his hair combed on the doorstep.*
> *"Don't pull like that. It's bad enough being touched.*
> *When you have done my hair, I shall have hated you."*
> *. . . "Don't pull so far on my hair . . ."*
>
> *And now let me be, I am going alone.*
> *. . . an insect is waiting to treat with me . . .*
> *Or else I have an alliance with blue-veined stones . . .*

I had long light-brown hair and shaggy bangs to my eyes. My sisters, blessed with straight hair, kept it short and brushed simply, parted and tied on top with a ribbon. But mine each morning must have every curl dampened and brushed into a coil about a finger.

"Ow."

"Hold still, Helga."

"Make Janet wait for me."

"She will. Stop wriggling."

"She won't. Nobody will. I'll be last. I wish I were a boy. Ow."

And I wore knickers and knee socks and a white shirt and dashed out to the swings in the yard. The wood seat was removable and I flung it out and sat on the rope as I liked to do, sailing high. There was a narrow tire for a swing also, from the Model-T Ford. And there were iron rings: small ones to take in the hands and swing that way; large ones from which to hang by the knees, hair mussed and dangling, pushing on the ground with the palms to start the motion. I shouted a song my father had got from his friend, Lloyd Lewis:

WHERE, OH WHERE IS OLD ELIJAH?

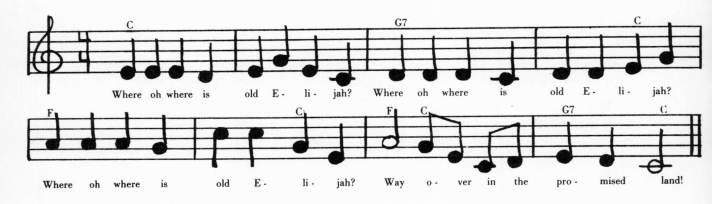

Where oh where is old E-li-jah? Where oh where is old E-li-jah? Where oh where is old E-li-jah? Way o-ver in the pro-mised land!

2

He went up in a fiery chariot;
By and by we will go and see him,
Way over in the promised land!

3

Where oh where are the Hebrew children?
They went up in a fiery furnace,
Way over in the promised land!

4

Where oh where is the bad boy Absalom?
He went up on the spear of Joab!
Way over in the promised land!

5

Where oh where is poor old Daniel?
He went up in a den of lions,
Way over in the promised land!

Our father had a bicycle and used to peddle away and be gone for an afternoon, traveling miles of country roads. I was occasionally set on the handlebars where, terrified, speechless to protest, preferring the security of the tricycles Janet and I rode, I was spun out into the close-by farmland, an old harmonizing song in my ears:

I FOUND A HORSESHOE

I found a horse-shoe; I found a horse-shoe I picked it up and nailed it on the door; And it was rus-ty and full of nail holes, Good luck 'twill bring to you for-ev-er more. Oh, the man who owned the horse he lived in New York, the man who owned the horse he lived in New York, The man who owned the horse, the man who owned the horse, The man who owned the horse he lived in New York.

2
The horse that wore the shoe his name was Mike,
The horse that wore the shoe his name was Mike,
The horse that wore the shoe, the horse that wore the shoe,
The horse that wore the shoe his name was Mike!

He could whistle wonderfully, sometimes in imitation of birds, quavering and trilling. And he sang:

EVERY TIME I COME TO TOWN

Eve-ry time I come to town the boys start a-kick-ing my dog a-round.

Makes no difference if he is a hound,
They got to quit kicking my dog around!

WHISTLE

2
They tied a tin can to his tail,
And drove him past the county jail;
Lem he cussed and Jim he swore
And that just naturally made me sore!
WHISTLE

People passed through the house, joining in the sings, and in the talking. I recall few; I was not involved. It is possible that I remember Eugene Debs and his kindly arms and how he lifted and carried me and how I sat on his knee and admired his bald head, when four years old or so. But it may only be that I have seen the photos in the album.

The songs remain more vivid, and the noise, the banter, and the serene tone of the household. I learned along with "Halleluia, I'm a Bum" and "The Big Rock Candy Mountain," songs that we sang as if they were light-hearted, one by a Wobbly songwriter, Swede by birth, who was arrested and indicted and shot to the ground at Salt Lake City, Utah, in November of 1915. Up and down the nation they used his tune:

YOU WILL EAT BYE AND BYE

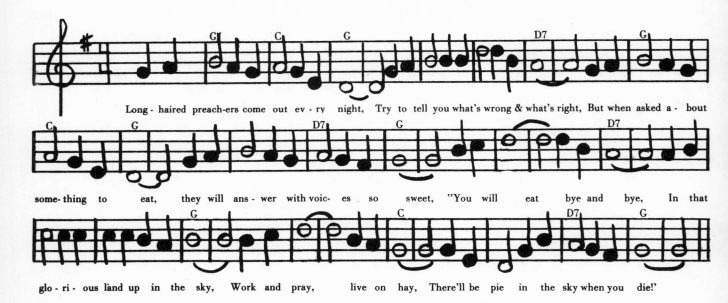

2
Workingmen of all countries unite,
Together we'll stand and we'll fight;
When the world and its wealth we have gained,
To the grafters we'll sing this refrain:
"You will eat bye and bye,
When you've learned how to cook and to fry,
Chop some wood, do you good,
And you'll eat in the sweet bye and bye!"

When the song's author was executed, *The New York Times* ran a two-page obituary, and a song almost as popular as the one he had written began going down and across and about the country:

JOE HILL

I dreamed I saw Joe Hill last night a-live as you and me. Says I, "But Joe, you're ten years dead." "I ne-ver died," says he. "I ne-ver died," says he!

2
"The copper bosses killed you, Joe; they shot you Joe," says I.
"Takes more than guns to kill a man,"
Says Joe, "I didn't die." Says Joe, "I didn't die."

3
And standing there as big as life, and smiling with his eyes,
Joe says, "What they forgot to kill
Went on to organize. Went on to organize.

4
"Joe Hill ain't dead," he says to me, "Joe Hill ain't never died.
Where working men are out on strike
Joe Hill is at their side, Joe Hill is at their side.

5
"From San Diego up to Maine, in every mine and mill
Where workers strike and organize,"
Says he, "You'll find Joe Hill." Says he, "You'll find Joe Hill."

6
I dreamed I saw Joe Hill last night alive as you and me.
Says I, "But Joe, you're ten years dead."
"I never died," says he. "I never died," says he!

I knew nothing of death, violent or otherwise. My sole encounter had been when I was three or four and played with the small sons of a family who lived down on the corner in a great house. Their grandmother was once put into an ambulance. There is the memory of the splendor of the event and the knowledge that death was nearby. And mingled in it is the comradeship for the youngest boy, round-faced and lisping, because he and I were still sent to take naps, being the "babies of the families."

We went to Sunday School. We weren't sent there or to church, but if we wished to go it was fine. We already knew spirituals. There

they didn't sing them in the morning class, but another kind of tune.
One was familiar to the childhood of almost every American:

JESUS LOVES ME

Je - sus loves me, this I know For the Bi - ble tells me so; Lit - tle ones to Him be - long;

They are weak, but He is strong. Yes, Je - sus loves me, yes, Je - sus loves me, Yes, Je - sus loves me, the Bi - ble tells me so!

2
Jesus loves me, He will stay
Close beside me all the way;
If I love Him, when I die
He will take me home on high.

Then on the way home, giggling, we whispered our parodies, the younger copying the elder ones, dumb before the adults:

I AM JESUS' LITTLE LAMB

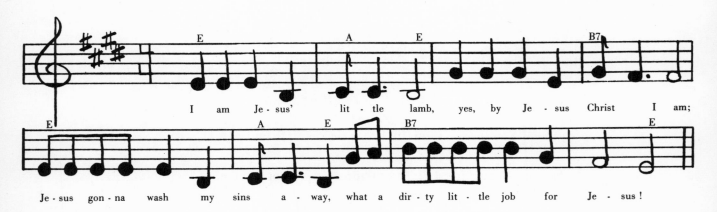

I am Je - sus' lit - tle lamb, yes, by Je - sus Christ I am;

Je - sus gon - na wash my sins a - way, what a dir - ty lit - tle job for Je - sus!

Some we inherited from the Salvation Army, and had heard them at our home, even rendered by visitors:

There's flies on you, flies on me, but there ain't no flies on Je - sus!

In the Sunday School we learned simple rhythmical songs and were taught to illustrate them, pointing and using the age-old gesture of sleep, the palms together against the tenderly bended head:

AWAY IN A MANGER

A - way in a man - ger, no crib for His bed, the lit - tle Lord Je - sus lay down His sweet head; the stars in the dark skies looked down where He lay, the lit - tle Lord Je - sus a - sleep on the hay.

2
The cattle are lowing; the poor baby wakes,
But little Lord Jesus no crying He makes;
I love Thee, Lord Jesus! Look down from the sky
And stay by my cradle till morning is nigh.

The head of our household had written:

The young child, Christ, is straight and wise
And asks questions of the old men . . .
And the old men answer nothing and only know love
For the young child Christ . . .

The spirituals had a separate kind of rhythm, which was adaptable to moods. They had been made for a purpose, rising slowly from a People's throat. They weren't reworked in the serenity of a study, but were formed in the quiet of green dusty slave fields. There men made an intimate personal philosophy, and changed the bitter to beauty.

In the South's nights the sky of stars was spread above. A small gray bird was singing concealed, the mockingbird, placed there for them, no other bird in all the States having its range and tone. The People started their songs, and then added and changed, condensed and borrowed, until each one was right. The songs became every American's. The Acts of the Apostles, Chapter sixteen, says

. . . And when they had laid many stripes upon them, they cast them into prison. . . . And at midnight Paul and Silas prayed, and sang praises unto God . . . And suddenly there was a great earthquake, so that the foundations of the prison were shaken: and immediately all the doors were opened, and everyone's bonds were loosed . . .

PAUL AND SILAS

Paul and Si - las bound in ja - il, all night long; One for to sing and the o - ther for to pray, all night long;

One for to sing and the o - ther for to pra - y, all night long; Do Lord, de - li - ver poor me!

2

Straight up to heaven and straight right back, all night long;
Ain't but the one train on this track, all night long;
Ain't but the one train on this track, all night long;
Do Lord, deliver poor me!

3

Never seen the like since I been born, all night. long;
People keep a-coming and the train done gone, all night long;
People keep a-coming and the train done gone, all night long;
Do Lord, deliver poor me!

Steichen, our Uncle Ed, our mother's only brother, came sometimes, bringing gifts. One time from France he handed me an enormous doll called Mary Jane, and two smaller ones for Janet, a pair,
Jack and Jill. These playthings were of felt fabric, with painted faces,
curled hair, un-American, distinctive. They became part of the growing clan of dolls.

Our uncle and father clowned for us; we roared with laughter,
helpless; weak, we flung ourselves on the rug at their feet. There was
no one so funny as those two. And arm in arm they would sing in
maundering tones, "Where Is My Wandering Boy Tonight?" and
"A Boy's Best Friend Is His Mother."

But there were times when we knew to let the two men alone.
It was when, in between the shouting and gaiety, there were the long
intense talking hours, so that once when we children were shown a
photograph of Abraham Lincoln, melancholy, we said it was our uncle.
But for us, on the visits, he got down on all fours, a dog, roaring,
attacking, involved in a highly dangerous fight with another dog.

I was expected to recite. "Swipes," the low voice summoned with
my nickname which had stuck, "come along in here and give us 'Opportunity.'"

"No," I called, hopeful of being asked again.

"For your uncle who will," he assured me, "reciprocate!"

I knew it well. It was by Edward Rowland Sill and called *Opportunity*.

> *. . . And men yelled, and swords*
> *Shocked upon swords and shields . . .*
> *Then came the king's son, wounded, sore bestead,*
> *And weaponless, and saw the broken sword,*
> *Hilt-buried in the dry and trodden sand,*
> *And ran and snatched it, and with battle-shout*
> *Lifted afresh he hewed his enemy down,*
> *And saved a great cause that heroic day!*

When it came the others' turn, our uncle recited *The Wreck of the Hesperus*, going the limit in histrionics, terrifying.

> *It was the schooner Hesperus,*
> *That sailed the wintry sea;*
> *And the skipper had taken his little daughter,*
> *To bear him company.*

Ending so that sometimes one burst into tears:

> *The salt sea was frozen on her breast,*
> *The salt tears in her eyes;*
> *And he saw her hair, like the brown sea-weed,*
> *On the billows fall and rise.*
> *Such was the wreck of the Hesperus,*
> *In the midnight and the snow!*
> *Christ save us all from a death like this,*
> *On the reef of Norman's Woe!*

"Did I ever tell you nieces," Steichen said, "of how I brought my mother over from Luxembourg? We went steerage. I was eighteen months old at the time, and it wasn't easy."

And then the two men tramped out of the house, to make long walks into the countryside. A few blocks out of the city the corn belt began, stretching from village to village, the railroad tracks sometimes leading right through a cornfield. They stopped in at small shops to buy popcorn or a draught of beer. Then they walked forth again, talking forever and ever, straightening out the world, the situation of the arts, and anything that came to their minds.

The next night the table talk might run onto unknowns. Jokes were recounted, ones that went over my disinterested head. Two men had just died and gone to the hereafter, one telling the other, "I say, heaven isn't so bad after Chicago." And the other, "Bill, this ain't heaven."

There was one about a man at a racetrack which hid its humor somewhere from me, for years. This was a superstitious man who never bet unless he received a sign. He had noted his parking ticket was number twenty. So was his seat number. He discovered twenty cents in change in his pocket. And overhead came a roaring airplane with a twenty on the wing. When a horse came up named Twenty Grand, he bet on him. Twenty Grand galloped in twenty leagues behind the rest of the field, and so the man stood up. He stamped on his hat in a rage and yelled, "God damn that fellow Roosevelt!"

I told a joke that was my style. A little boy loved the statue of General Grant on his horse. But his mother said they must leave because his father had a job in another city. The little boy had been visiting the statue as often as he could, morning and night. "We'll take one last look," said his mother, "and then we must really go." They stood there and the little boy said, "Mama, who is the man on top of General Grant?"

And always the songs in the evenings:

TWO WHITE HORSES

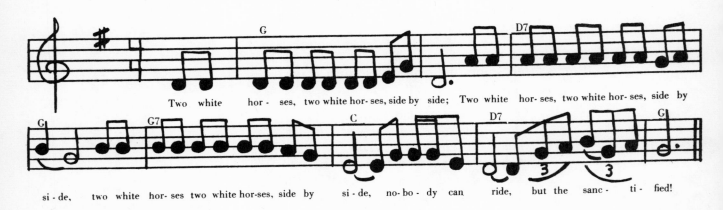

Two white hor - ses, two white hor-ses, side by side; Two white hor - ses, two white hor-ses, side by si - de, two white hor - ses two white hor-ses, side by si - de, no-bo - dy can ride, but the sanc - ti - fied!

2
Daniel was a man, Daniel was a man, in the lion's den,
The good Lord proved to be Daniel's friend!

3
Zekiel was a man, Zekiel was a man, and he rassled with sin,
Heaven's gate opened wide, and Zekiel rolled right in!

Far back in the summers of that once upon a time, my sisters and mother and I went to a resort up in Wisconsin, to Williams Bay or Lake Geneva; or to Lake Michigan. When our father was able, he joined us. The communities then were loosely organized or not at all. There was plenty of room, some were almost wilderness. I was jumbled over bumpy roads with my sisters in the back seat of a narrow-tired Model-T. Along the way we bought towering rainbow ice-cream cones and rendered, high and happy:

DUBLIN BAY

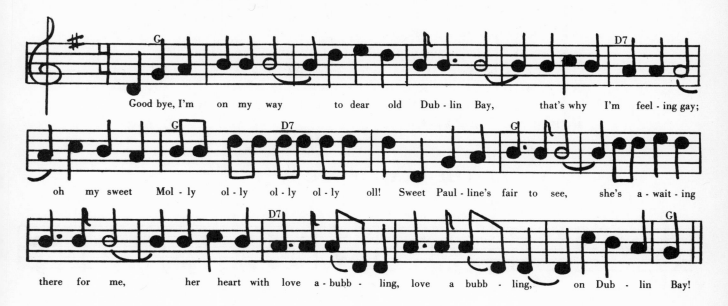

Good bye, I'm on my way to dear old Dub - lin Bay, that's why I'm feel - ing gay; oh my sweet Mol - ly ol - ly ol - ly ol - ly oll! Sweet Paul - line's fair to see, she's a - wait - ing there for me, her heart with love a - bubb - ling, love a bubb - ling, on Dub - lin Bay!

Occasionally we got carsick and a bathing cap came in handy. The houses we stayed in were tall-ceilinged wood structures with sand gritting on the bare floors. In the kitchens were ice safes that smelled of earth and must, and always leaked. In the upstairs rooms were iron bedsteads and rigid chairs. Outside was a bare porch and there were old trees and sun and grass, a sandy road down to the water. We wore striped wool bathing suits all day long, when in the water were buoyed up by thin tire tubes and in time learned to dog-paddle and to swim and to stay under, our strokes our own, individual. The hired girl went along, for everyone had a girl, a member of the family, who imparted as much of her wisdom and her disenchantments to the children as the missus of the household. Often more, for she came from a less tender home. She didn't swim with us, but was there to oversee. In a long dress with bloused sleeves, white stockings, black shoes, and a cloche hat. Sometimes she taught us a tender tune that the family took over for their own:

OLD DOG TRAY

Old dog Tray's ev - er faith - ful, Grief can - not drive him a - way; he is gen - tle, he is kind; I'll nev - er, nev - er find a bet - ter friend than old dog Tray!

And then when the endless summertime was over, we returned to our home. The small brown-and-white dog followed me up the stairway where I went to see whether the dolls were safe, to dress the favorite in her nightgown and put her in her crib, solicitous.

Then I stayed at the stairhead and heard the family talking down below. After a while the guitar strummed, and I leaned on the wall, listening. Soon, curled on the floor boards, I was sleeping, in my arms my brown-and-white pet.

WHERE THE PRAITIES GROW

Oh, have you been in love, me boys, and have you felt the pain? I'd rather be in jail, me boys, than be in love a- gain; I met her in the mor-ning, and I'll have youse all to know, that I met her in the gar-den where the prai- ties grow!

2
And now that we are married,
And are blessed with children three,
The girls just like their mother,
And the boys the image of me;
We'll bring them up so sweetly
In the way they ought to grow,
So they'll ne'er forget the garden
Where the praities grow!

PART TWO

. . . My mother, clothed in the setting sun,
put away her youth in a deep guitar,
and only on certain evenings would she show
it to her children,
sheathed in music, light, and words . . .
—JORGE CARRERA ANDRADE

Songs run like patchwork threads through life. Some stamp a moment so thereafter they can't be freed from it, and return the essence of it whenever the song is heard. Nostalgia is wound and fastened about songs; the pang of the lost past of childhood or of an old love remains, stubborn, with the tune that belongs to it.

And songs are the property of a people, a nation, an area, a state. I had been taught a patriotic song as soon as I'd entered first grade:

ILLINOIS

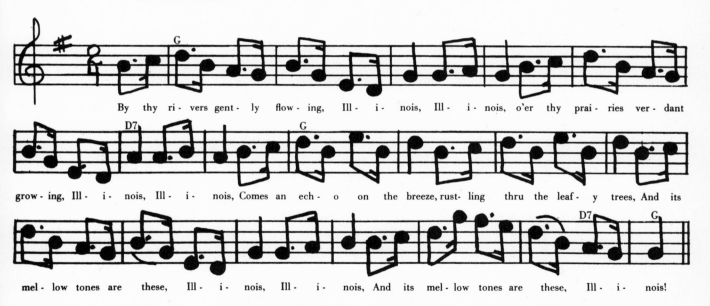

By thy ri - vers gent - ly flow - ing, Ill - i - nois, Ill - i - nois, o'er thy prai - ries ver - dant growing, Ill - i - nois, Ill - i - nois, Comes an ech - o on the breeze, rust - ling thru the leaf - y trees, And its mel - low tones are these, Ill - i - nois, Ill - i - nois, And its mel - low tones are these, Ill - i - nois!

2
Not without thy wondrous story, Illinois, Illinois,
Can be writ the nation's glory, Illinois, Illinois,
On the record of thy years, Abraham Lincoln's name appears,
Grant and Logan, and our tears, Illinois, Illinois,
Grant and Logan, and our tears, Illinois!

And then when I was nine, my family was emigrating from Illinois over to the sand dune territory of southwest Michigan. I began walking a mile a day out to the highway to catch a school bus. With the new classmates, children of farmers and small townspeople, I learned my new patriotic song:

MICHIGAN, MY MICHIGAN

A song to thee, fair state of mine, Mi- chi- gan, my Mi- chi- gan; But great- er song than this is thine, Mi- chi- gan, my Mi- chi- gan; The whis- per of the for- est tree, the thun- der of the in- land sea; U- nite in one grand sym- pho- ny; Mi- chi- gan, my Mi- chi- gan!

2

Thou rich in wealth that makes a state, Michigan, my Michigan;
Thou great in things that make us great, Michigan, my Michigan;
Our loyal voices sound thy claim upon the golden roll of fame,
Our loyal hands shall write the name of Michigan, my Michigan.

On top of a towering bare sandhill was the high rambling house our mother designed for us. Clever with blueprints, she had already built two cottages on a creek further up the lake where we first came to visit in summers. This tall house was on the north border of a once-fashionable summer resort, Birchwood Beech, now quiet. A small loyal group of Chicago people came out regularly to rent the tiny cabins and unheated frame buildings. Our mother hired a local carpenter who, lonely, carried the long beams on his shoulders, not requiring any assistance. His sons were babies then and he waited on the day in later years when, true to guild traditions, they would carry his beams and take up his trade.

Into the cellar of the house was built a dank-smelling, gloomy concrete-and-steel vault, to protect books and manuscripts from fire. It had the flavor of Edgar Allan Poe's tales. There was a combination scratched somewhere to open the great door. My fingers had memorized it; always I was called upon when the door accidentally locked and everyone forgot where the combination was noted. As soon as I began turning the knob, the numbers came back to me, and the tumblers slid loosely into place. I would get claustrophobia when working in there, set at some task for our father, filing or hunting books or arranging the pasteboard cartons of clippings and papers and sometimes a bust of him or a plaque in honor. Shelves lined the place, and high metal oblong First War army trunks stood about. Sometimes playing games with friends in the cellar, we hid in there, caught by its mood and its musty odor, grave-like!

The home was full of windows and the sun gazed in. On the brick terrace out in front stood weathered chairs. There over the years we watched the progression of sunsets, all incredible, running the gamut from gray serenity to a blazing like Resurrection Day.

It was a violent country. The huge lake was treacherous and so was the land. It was the Walking Dune country, where the sand moved almost imperceptibly, the landscape continually changing. From some sand mound, the top branches of a giant oak would protrude like arms of a drowning man. And tumbleweeds were always speeding by in the late season, hurled by the wind to somewhere else. Most of the dune trees and bushes were young, a character of deserts. The convex sides of the dunes faced the lake where the winds came and drove them inland, or wandering this way or that.

Early, in love with the country, we girls had no fear. We swam when we pleased, if ice floes were on the lake in early spring, or if it were the black of night and the shore were indistinguishable from the horizon. We dared danger. When electrical storms started in summer, and the hot sky over the water darkened, and the air turned purple-colored, and lightning began to flash, thunder to mutter, we put on our suits. Sweating, we dashed down the dune-side, the dogs at our heels, to plunge into the lake. There we stayed as the needling rain began. We shouted, the dogs barked. Then as the downpour continued, chilled, we trotted through the caking wet sand, up the dune stairway, and home, yelling, unthoughtful of the words:

MY SISTER SHE WORKS IN THE LAUNDRY

My sis-ter she works in the laun-dry, my da-ddy fi-ddles for gin, my mo-ther takes in wash-ing, Great God how the mon-ey rolls in!

In dry shorts and old shirts, to the music of rain, on the screened porch we sang. One song was had from the mother of an aunt who had

staked a claim in the Oklahoma Land Rush, in the late eighties, galloping on her horse with the rest. She said they used it there:

ROSIE NELL

How oft I dream of child-hood days and tricks we used to play Up - on each oth - er when at school to pass the time a way; they of - ten wished me with them but they al - ways wished in vain, I'd ra - ther be with Ro - sie Nell, a - swing - ing in the lane!

CHORUS
Swinging in the lane, swinging in the lane,
I'd rather be with Rosie Nell, swinging in the lane,
Swinging in the lane, swinging in the lane,
I'd rather be with Rosie Nell, swinging in the lane!

2
But soon a cloud of sorrow came, a strange young man from town
Was introduced to Rosie Nell by Aunt Jemima Brown;
She stayed away from school next day, the truth to me was plain:
She'd gone off with that city chap, swinging in the lane.

3
Now all young men with tender hearts, pray take advice from me,
Don't be so quick to fall in love with every girl you see,
For if you do, you soon will find, you've only loved in vain,
She'll go off with some other chap, swinging in the lane!

Years later, when I got to writing my third novel, it was almost
an excuse to tell of the love affair between me and the dunelands. And
I put in the children and the water and the dogs and the raft and the
songs:

A crowd of teen-agers were bringing the raft back for the last time
of the year. When there was a storm, the strong current, ignoring the drag
of the cinder-block anchor, would sometimes wash the raft a mile down
the shore, grounding it up on the beach. Then the Ardway boys would
bring shovels and spades, and the children trudge in a group down to dig
it out and bring it back. They came shouting, Alan's dogs accompanying
them along the shore. They pushed the ponderous wood thing against the

southeast-running waves. When the children got tired, they lay on it while the others shoved. They sang duets unless they got the giggles and the boys dumped them in the water:

Down at the sta - tion ear - ly in the morn - ing

In summers we rummaged about in the sand dunes, collecting arrowheads chipped out by old red-skinned clever hunters once, and we filled the shelves and drawers and corners of our rooms with fossils, crinoids embedded in brown stone, ovals and shells or the outline of some primaeval fish. At night, now and then, fog horns sounded raucous from the ports up the lake, their harsh notes amplified by the thick mist.

In winters there were the farm children with whom I went to school. Some were Teutonic. I knew the German tongue; it was spoken in my house sometimes when the Luxembourg grandmother, Oma, visited. Our mother and she spoke rapid Luxembourg and German, and cried to us to take our dolls and dogs and get out into the sunshine. We hung about them, listening, trying to decipher their secrets.

"Heraus. Aus dem haus!"

From the school children I heard an old song.

DER LINDENBAUM

Am Brun - nen vor der To - re da steht ein Lin - den - baum; Ich tra - umt' in sei - nem

Schat - ten so man - chen sus - sen Traum. Ich schnitt in sei - ne Rin - de so man - ches lie - be

Wort; es zog in Freud' und Lei - de zu ih - m mich i - mmer fort.

By the well outside the gateway there stands a Linden tree;
Beneath its sheltering branches the sweetest dreams came to me.
Upon its bark I've carven the dearest names I know;
And though I roam I must return in happiness and woe.

We named our home Pawpaw Patch, after the small engaging trees that crowded on the sandy slopes, the fruit banana-like, the leaves like great mittens or gloves; from the twigs hung the chrysalises of the Swallowtail butterflies for their caterpillars fancied the Pawpaw leaves.

There were always family dogs underfoot, who were photographed with a nestling cat or one of our baby-dolls, which they accepted gingerly, resigned. The exploits of the dogs, their fights and their adventures, were a part of our life. When Bosco, our first big German Shepherd, ran away with the hatchet, everybody was involved. He dashed first to the beach to bury it. Then when he glimpsed his pursuers, he dug it up and ran off again, circling over the bluff, and when sighted approaching home in a few minutes, came gay, wagging his brush.

We pleaded, "Bosco, help us find the hatchet!"

But he refused, and enjoyed accompanying the searchers. Finally our mother found the spot where sand was disturbed and there were fresh Bosco tracks. Underneath the tool was revealed. "Oh, Bosco." He leaped about with unfeigned joy.

We hailed the happening. Two of the dogs disliked each other violently; they had an intense and secret rivalry, so that gates must be set up to separate them. But when the latch was inevitably left undone, there would be a snarling scramble and someone got bitten, usually myself because one of the dogs would be my special charge. Then wounds were washed and peace again maintained for a while. We didn't think of rabies then; dog bites were as acceptable as skinned knees. We exhibited them as evidence of our maturing, proud.

And we respected the dogs for their tenacity and heroism, dressed their torn skin, as they stood licking their fresh scars. There were three of the German Shepherds at one time, Bosco and his sons, Jojo and Frisco; and there were a pair of Irish Setters, particular pets of our father, Cully and Dan. And a white Collie, Benaboy, who was mine by mutual understanding; and various mongrels, one extraordinary, the son of Benaboy and a neighboring German Shepherd bitch; he was Jack.

I was determined to make dogs my business, and drew up blueprints for future kennels, organized local dog shows, schooled my own flock of four or five to leap barriers and hoops, to draw sulky carts or in the winters, in tandem teams, to pull sleds over the arctic landscape. "Mush!" And they were trained to climb trees, too; I had a gang of them standing in the branches of some tree upon my demand. Their enthusiasm matched my own. "Up. Jump!"

And there were tame white and piebald rats for pets; and I put on a show of them, with miniature pens and bedding of sawdust. There was a succession of crows, baby owls and hawks, a Canada Goose, a raccoon, dull-witted oppossums, and of course, rabbits, guinea pigs, cats.

All of these projects were interrupted always by the ending of vacations and the beginning of school. I got on well with my country classmates, liking Dutch, who was short and jolly and not so bright, the same as Hank who was ugly and tall and shared honors with me at the top of the class one year. Out in our schoolyard was a great round swing which circled a steel pole; twenty could sit on the seat as it whirled, clanging against the pole, surging, so I was sometimes seasick again. Unknowing of the terror of the songs I sometimes sang, I shouted a rhythmic one I'd learned at home:

TELL OLD BILL

2

Bill left home by the garden gate this morning,
Bill left home by the garden gate this evening,
Bill left home by the garden gate;
Old Sal says, "Now don't be late!"
This morning, this evening, so soon.

3

Bill's wife was baking bread this morning . . .
When she got word that Bill was dead,
This morning, this evening, so soon.

4

"Oh dear, that can't be so, this morning . . .
'Cause Bill left home about an hour ago,
This morning, this evening, so soon.

5

"Oh dear, that cannot be, this morning . . .
They shot my husband in the first degree,
This morning, this evening, so soon!"

6

They brought Bill home in the hurry-up wagon, this morning . . .
And when they brought him home his toes was dragging,
This morning, this evening, so soon.

In school I wore respectable girl's clothes. When a dress or sweater or pair of shoes pleased our mother, she got two or three more of the same. And so when she liked the fit of a certain dirndl polka-dot frock on Janet and me, she got us each a green, a red, and a blue. They were strong of fabric and the hems were deep and they lasted, to my dismay, eternally.

Each day when I reached home, I changed into familiar tomboy clothes. They suited me, knickers and a sweater or shirt in cool weather, a gym suit in summer. I was an addict one year to the Tarzan books, and at home spent time in trees. With friends I built platforms in the branches, and passed days shouting the ape man's calls from there, passed nights sleeping in blankets beneath the tree. When Tarzan was played out, I turned to other jungle folk. And after a while came upon Sherlock Holmes. He took a winter.

Our local library was lodged in a museum donated to the town by a beneficent lover of the countryside, who had also given over a woods nearby for the pleasure of bird watchers, nature people, horse-back riders, and lovers. When I was in the eighth grade I went to the museum one day, bent on exploring the glass cases of dead birds and lepidoptera, and the exhibits of shells and arrowheads. There in the dingy window was a display which stopped me: two medals and two pins, to be awarded by the American Legion to a boy and girl possessing virtues of "courage, character, service, companionship, and scholarship," to a high degree. On the face of the medal my eyes fastened to was a noble woman grasping a flag and all about her were the words: FOR GOD AND COUNTRY. My desire was strong.

Secretly I studied with greater care, fearful of my luck, despairing of my mathematical and confident of my literary ability. And at the season's end, clad in a blue polka-dot dirndl dress that now reached above my knees, I accepted in self-conscious agony, to scattered applause, the medal and pin. I bore them home to my unimpressed family.

They raised their eyebrows, "The American Legion, Helga?"

But I took the prizes to my room and put them in my drawer, the secret triumph unimpaired. I changed to knickers and jacket and went out to hunt for uncommon trees and bushes and plants, to build up the collection of leaves our mother had started, and wild flowers. Scouring the tomes the family had gathered on the subject, we spent hours identifying them. Birds were spotted too, as they came and went. Warblers and odd fowl, loons and the like, moved through in the migrating seasons. I made lists.

We weren't lonely, though our house stood isolate. We knew the words of our poet in the house:

> *There is a music for lonely hearts nearly always.*
> *If the music dies down there is a silence*
> *Almost the same as the movement of music.*
> *To know silence perfectly is to know music.*

And sang:

I'M SAD AND I'M LONELY

I'm sad and I'm lone-ly, my heart it will break; my sweet-heart loves an-o-ther, Lord I wish I was dead!

2
My cheeks once were red as the bud on the rose,
But now they are whiter than the lily that grows.

3
I'll build me a cabin on a mountain so high,
Where the blackbirds can't see me or hear my sad cry.

4
I'm troubled, I'm troubled, I'm troubled in mind,
And if trouble don't kill me, I'll live a long time!

One summer I learned of revolution and terror, sitting cross-legged with others down at the beach. Someone had a guitar and we were looking at the sunset. Our damp bathing suits were scratchy from sand, and a cooling offshore breeze was starting up as the land temperature dropped and moved out upon the yet warm surface water. The ball of dying sun fell into its pool of blood across the lake, upon the horizon.

We were singing a tune we'd sung over and over on other nights. But at that moment I was listening for the first time to the words. What had been a catchy melody became live history. It was a song that had been used by strong men who would not be swayed from their stand against tyrants. A young fellow had been hanged in a Dublin prison yard on 1 November 1920; the English had not yet granted Home Rule or recognized the Free State, and Ireland was martyred. The song's hero had enlisted in the Republican Army and been captured in ambush.

KEVIN BARRY

Ear-ly on a Mon-day mor-ning, high up-on the gal-lows tree, Ke-vin Ba-rry gave his young life for the cause of li-ber-ty.

2

Only a lad of eighteen summers,
Still there's no one can deny
As he walked to death that morning
Nobly held his head up high.

3

Another martyr for old Ireland,
Another murder for the crown,
Brutal laws to crush the Irish
Could not keep their spirits down.

4

Lads like Barry are no cowards,
From their foes they do not fly;
And their bravery always has been
Ireland's cause to live or die!

5

"Kevin Barry, do not leave us,
On the scaffold you must die,"
Cried his brokenhearted mother
As she bade her son goodbye.

6

Kevin turned to her in silence
Saying, "Mother, do not weep,
For it's all for dear old Ireland
And it's all for freedom's sake!"

7

Just before he faced the hangman
In his lonely prison cell,
The Black and Tans they tortured Barry
Just because he wouldn't tell

8

The names of his brave comrades
And other things they wished to know.
"Turn informer and we'll free you."
But Kevin proudly answered, "No!

9

"Shoot me like a soldier,
Do not hang me like a dog,
For I fought to free old Ireland
On that still September morn,

10

"All around the little bakery
Where we fought them hand to hand.
Shoot me like a brave soldier
For I fought for Ireland!"

And then the Negro cook of one of the families sang a spiritual that was exciting to everyone. She had to be coaxed and we wouldn't let her go:

I HAVE GOT RELIGION

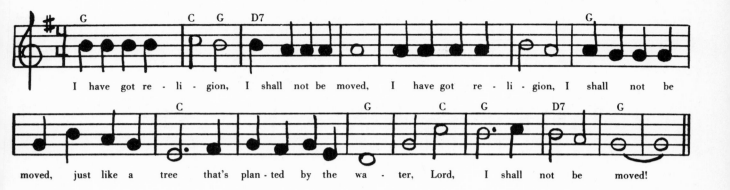

I have got re - li - gion, I shall not be moved, I have got re - li - gion, I shall not be
moved, just like a tree that's plan - ted by the wa - ter, Lord, I shall not be moved!

2
I'm going to meet my mother, I shall not be moved,
I'm going to meet my mother, I shall not be moved,
Just like a tree that's planted by the water,
I shall not be moved.

It was from Jeremiah:
*Blessed is the man that trusteth in the Lord, and whose hope the
Lord is. For he shall be as a tree planted by the waters.*
The unions about the country were using the tune for their pur-
poses. Though not involved in their unhappiness, we sang their song:

WE SHALL NOT BE MOVED

The Union is behind us, we shall not be moved,
The Union is behind us, we shall not be moved,
Just like a tree that's planted by the water,
Lord, we shall not be moved!

We're fighting for our freedom . . .

We're fighting for our children . . .

We'll build a mighty Union . . .

And they sang too:
The Union gives us beans, bacon and potatoes . . .
Or in derision:

So-and-so is a horse-thief, he shall be removed,
So-and-so is a horse-thief, he shall be removed,
Just like the empty glasses on the table
He shall be removed!

From verses in Genesis came a gospel song of the South, which
we sang. Twenty-eighth chapter, verses ten to twelve:
And Jacob went out from Beersheba, and went toward Haran . . . and he
dreamed, and behold a ladder set up on the earth, and the top of it reached
to heaven: and behold the angels of God ascending and descending on it.

WE ARE CLIMBING JACOB'S LADDER

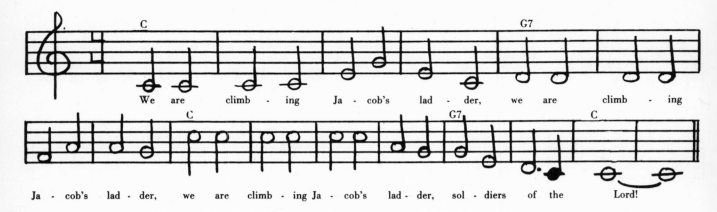

We are climb-ing Ja-cob's lad-der, we are climb-ing Ja-cob's lad-der, we are climb-ing Ja-cob's lad-der, sol-diers of the Lord!

Every rung goes higher, higher . . .

Sinner, do you love my Jesus? . . .

If you love Him, why not serve Him? . . .

Praise God, bring out the glory, glory,
Praise God, bring out the glory, glory,
Praise God, bring out the glory, glory,
Soldiers of the cross!

We heard of the pickets in the nights, with campfires lit, who chanted, changing the lines easily, calling, "Amen, brother," to the labor organizers. The rain fell; weeks went by. The strikes would be lost and the unions finished. But still they sang, in their homes and meeting places:

WE ARE BUILDING A STRONG UNION

We are building a strong union,
We are building a strong union,
We are building a strong union,
Workers in the mill!

Every member makes us stronger . . .

Some day we shall gain the victory . . .

The miners in West Virginia heard of it and took it up:

We have toiled through dark and danger,
We have toiled through dark and danger,
We have toiled through dark and danger,
Workers in the mine!

Though we work hard, we are starving . . .

The lake beside which we sat and sang stayed my constant companion for almost two decades. When I left high school I refused to go to college for a few years, unable to leave the water. I had a devotion to it as though it were some silent demanding animal that was mine, and would miss me if I were gone. When in later years I returned to see if there were changes, I would hurry, urgent, to stop and stand and stare at the meadow of water, in constant love.

Sometimes there were drownings and crowds would slowly gather to stand about the bloated thing until the ambulance men came to carry it off. The water raged in changing seasons like a dangerous fabled monster, undomesticated, charming. All this wildness attached one to the lake, half-wary, half-fearful, enchanted.

There was a song we sang of a ship upon our inland sea:

BIGERLOW

It was one Oc-to-ber mor-ning that I seen a won-drous sight; it was the tim-ber dro-ver Bi-ger-low a-hail-ing from De-troit. Watch her! catch her, jump up in her ju-ju-ba-ju! give her the sheet and let her go, we're the boys to see her through, you should of heard her how-ling, when the wind was blow-ing free, it was on the trip to Buf-fa-lo from Mil-wau-kee!

And we were singing of the lake when the ditty went:

LIFE ON THE OCEAN WAVE

Life on the o-cean wave a home on the rol-ling deep, the wife she won't be-have and the ba-by won't go to sleep!

The body of water stormed and surged. Ice mounds, tall and treacherous, bordered the winter lake, as the waves dashed upon those already formed, building them higher and yet higher. We tramped along the shore, the snow mixed with sand underfoot, and if it blew, it stung as the silica grains and sleet dashed and whirled. We sang into the gale:

STEAMBOAT BILL

Down the Mississippi steamed the Whippoorwill, commanded by the pilot Mr. Steamboat Bill, the owner gave him orders on the strict Q. T., to try to beat the record of the Robert E. Lee.

CHORUS
Steamboat Bill, sailing down the Mississippi, Steamboat Bill, a mighty man was he; Steamboat Bill, sailing down the Mississippi, gonna try to beat the record of the Robert E. Lee.

CHORUS
Steamboat Bill, sailing down the Mississippi,
Steamboat Bill, he's with an angel band,
Steamboat Bill, sailing down the Mississippi,
He's a pilot on a steamboat in the Promised Land.

2
"So, feed up your fires, let the old smoke blow,
Burn up all your cargo if we run out of coal,
We gotta beat the record," says Billy to the mate,
"Or the early mail'll beat us to the Golden Gate!"

3
Up stepped a gambling man from Louisville,
Tried to get a bet against the *Whippoorwill.*
Bill flashed a roll that surely was a bear,
When the boiler that exploded blew them up in the air.

4

The gambler says to Bill as they left the wreck,
"I don't know where we're going, but we're neck and neck."
Says Bill to the gambler, "I'll tell you what I'll do,
I'll bet a hundred thousand dollars I go higher than you!"

The history in the songs escaped me. The songs seemed fiction, well-told tales, not related to fact. Only in later years would I know that it was from rugged fact often that songs were born. One of our fine bold favorites, with a rousing Irish tune, was a ballad of a trip down three of the Great Lakes:

RED IRON ORE

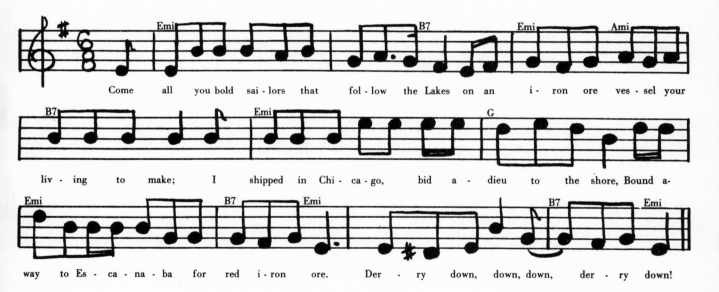

Come all you bold sai-lors that fol-low the Lakes on an i-ron ore ves-sel your liv-ing to make; I shipped in Chi-ca-go, bid a-dieu to the shore, Bound a-way to Es-ca-na-ba for red i-ron ore. Der-ry down, down, down, der-ry down!

2

In the month of September, the seventeenth day,
Two dollars and a quarter is all they would pay,
And on Monday morning the *Bridgeport* did take
The *E. C. Roberts* out in the Lake.
Derry down, down, down derry down!

3

The wind from the southward sprang up a fresh breeze
And away through Lake Michigan the *Roberts* did sneeze,
Down through Lake Michigan the *Roberts* did roar,
And on Friday morning we passed through death's door.

4

This packet she howled across the mouth of Green Bay,
And before her cutwater she dashed the white spray;
We rounded the sand point, our anchor let go,
We furled in our canvas and the watch went below.

53

5

Next morning we hove alongside the *Exile*,
And soon was made fast to an iron ore pile,
They lowered their chutes and like thunder did roar,
They spouted into us that red iron ore.

6

Some sailors took shovels while others got spades,
And some took wheelbarrows, each man to his trade;
We looked like red devils, our fingers got sore,
We cursed Escanaba and that damned iron ore.

7

The tug *Escanaba* she towed out the *Minch*,
The *Roberts* she thought she had left in a pinch,
And as she passed by us she bid us goodbye,
Saying, "We'll meet you in Cleveland next Fourth of July!"

8

Through Louse Island it blew a fresh breeze;
We made the Foxes, the Beavers, the Skillageles;
We flew by the *Minch* for to show her the way,
And she never hove in sight till we were off Thunder Bay.

9

Across Saginaw Bay the *Roberts* did ride
With the dark and deep water rolling over her side;
And now for Port Huron the *Roberts* must go,
Where the tug *Kate Williams* she took us in tow.

10

We went through North Passage; Oh Lord, how it blew!
And all around the Dummy a large fleet there came too.
The night being dark, Old Nick it would scare,
We hove up next morning and for Cleveland did steer.

11

Now the *Roberts* is in Cleveland, made fast stem and stern,
And over the bottle we'll spin a big yarn;
But Captain Harvey Shannon had ought to stand treat
For getting into Cleveland ahead of the fleet.

12

Now my song is ended, I hope you won't laugh;
Our dunnage is packed and all hands are paid off;
Here's a health to the *Roberts*, she's staunch, strong and true;
Not forgotten the bold boys that comprise her crew.
Derry down, down, down derry down!

We had an Indiana cook that I adored. She wore starched sunbonnets to protect her fair skin when she worked for long outside. She had blonde soft hair and blue eyes. I watched her suitors come and go. Early she advised me, in her country tradition, to get a hope chest and beginning filling it, to embroider pillowcases, to occasionally add another Fostoria crystal glass to it, and thus to combat the probable lean income of my early married days.

I had no idea then of how I would ever snare a husband, despaired within myself of any possibility. I knew wonderful plaintive love songs that had no connection with reality. I sang often of the lover dead:

HE WAS THE WORLD TO ME

He went from his pa-lace grand, and he came to my cot-tage door; his words were few, but his looks, they will linger for-ever more. The smile in his sa - d dark eyes, more ten-der than wor-ds could be, though I was nothing to him, still he was the wor-ld to me!

2
Today in his palace grand
On a flower-strewn bier he lies,
With his beautiful lids fast closed
On his beautiful sad dark eyes.
Of all the mourners who mourn,
Why should I a mourner be?
For I was nothing to him,
Though he was the world to me!

Romantically, vaguely, our only real-life specimens of heroes being the sons of the owner of the nearby movie-house, and our book heroes being impossibly swaggering and grand, out of Scott and Dumas, we dreamed, schizophrenic:

SOMEBODY'S TALL AND HANDSOME

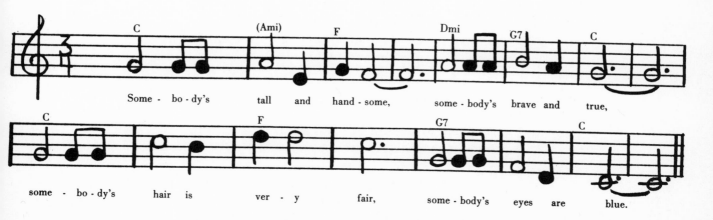

Some - bo - dy's tall and hand - some, some - body's brave and true, some - bo - dy's hair is ver - y fair, some - body's eyes are blue.

2

Somebody came to see me,
Somebody came last night,
Somebody asked me to marry him,
Of course I said, "All right!"

We sang of lovers and their problems:

ONE MORNING IN MAY

One morn-ing, one morn-ing, one morn-ing in May, I met a fair cou-ple a-mak-ing their way; One was a mai-den so bright and so fair, and the o-ther was a sol-dier and a brave vol-un-teer.

2

"Good morning, good morning, good morning to thee,
Oh, where are you going, my pretty lady?"
"Oh, I am a-going to the banks of the sea,
To see the waters gliding, hear the nightingales sing."

3

We hadn't been standing but a minute or two,
When out of his knapsack a fiddle he drew,
And the tune that he played made the valleys all ring,
Oh see the waters gliding, hear the nightingales sing.

4

"Pretty lady, pretty lady, it's time to give o'er."
"Oh no, pretty soldier, please play one tune more,
I'd rather hear your fiddle or the touch of one string,
Than to see the waters gliding, hear the nightingales sing.

5

"Pretty soldier, pretty soldier, will you marry me?"
"Oh no, pretty lady, that never can be;
I've a wife in old London and children twice three,
Two wives in the army's too many for me.

6

"I'll go back to old London and stay there one year,
And often I'll think of you, my little dear,
And if ever I return, 'twill be in the spring
To see the waters gliding, hear the nightingales sing!"

I had always liked housekeeping, and the cook took me in hand. "Every girl must know how to iron a man's shirt, Helga."

It somehow tied me in with a future I hoped against hope for. "Okay. Teach me." And she went through the steps.

"Now, you ought to learn how to run the wash machine. And to sort the clothes."

I began to ask for privileges. "Can I hang out the clothes this week? Please!"

"If you'll stretch the sheets properly. You hung them crooked last time, Helga."

"I'll do it right if it kills me."

And I stood in the yellow sun, my dogs and the huge wicker basket of sheets beside me, the clothespins in the pocket of the apron I wore over my knickers. I recited poetry, "Paul Revere's Ride," or some ballad of Browning whom I saw eye to eye with. And I sang what I'd heard our cook's farmer swain render over and over, with good-hearted determination:

SEVEN LONG YEARS

Se - ven long years in state pri - son, se - ven long years for to stay, for knock - ing a man down the al - ley and tak - ing his gold watch and chain. Sad sad and lone - ly, sit - ing in my lit - tle cell all a - lone, all a - lone, thinking of days that's gone by me and days when I have done wrong!

2
I wish I had the wings of a sparrow,
I wish I had the wings for to fly,
I would fly to the side of my mother
And there let me lay down and die.

I returned to the house, and my mother looked at me from her desk. "If you're ever in trouble and need money when you're grown, you can certainly housekeep!"

"Sure." From the corner I took my butterfly net and jar of cyanide. I liked her admiration; the security of a professional trade appealed to me; housekeeping would leave the mind free, a valued aspect. Later when I took to farming I liked it for the same reason. Out in the fields driving the team to the manure spreader, cleaning the stables, or milking the animals, I could memorize, recite, work up my own poems and think through ideas for my journal.

After lunch, with the clothes folded and put away, I went with Margaret to the tennis court, to play set after set in the blistering sun, and then exhausted return for our bathing suits and a swim. Our relationship was mainly an amiable one. Sometimes we fought though, verbally, screaming taut from one end of the room to the other. "I can't stand you! And you've got it all wrong!" Then later we made up.

By nature, the role of listener suited me. But Margaret was made differently. Now and then she took up her role of the Voice of The Opposition; she would get into a heavy skirmish, occasionally establish a victory, or again defeated, retire to the accompaniment of loud-banged doors. As an appeaser, I remained her steady admirer.

In the sultry long summer afternoons we trooped down to the cool of the cellar, made up a freezer-can of ice cream, someone driving the old Ford out to the nearby village for a gunny sack of ice. It was crushed with a mallet or the side of a hammer head, and packed with rock salt about the metal can which stood in the wood freezer bucket. Everyone took turns at the handle, and when it was stiff and ready we ladled it out into soup bowls with a huge iron spoon, sometimes the cream being tainted with the rock salt. The rest of the ice was heaped about the can to keep the ice cream frozen, and the smelly brown sack folded on top. The bucket was shoved back into the damp jam cellar or wood supply room; the ice cream must be finished before the day was over or it would melt.

We carried our bowls and separated, retiring outside under a tree, or to a low window somewhere to read whatever suited the fancy from the shelves that extended from cellar to roof, zigzagging through the house. Later the books would overflow into barns and milk houses as they were built, and then between milkings or garden work one could go to the dusty lofts to browse.

In summers there were companions in plenty among the summer resorters and we played violently, getting our fill. The season was short and the moment the newcomers would arrive, we descended upon them, if possible at the instant their car braked at their cottage. We help them unload or clutched our friend of last year by the hand and begged the parents to let him come at once with us.

There were afternoons spent on the raft built by the community, out on the lake. There were long evenings spent at poker with heaped bowls of popcorn, salted and buttered, and dishes of the chocolate fudge I made. Or a great chocolate cake, baked as I'd learned from my ally, the Indiana cook, in a huge oblong roaster-pan, and topped with thick swirled heavy fudge, and cut in squares. And there were treasure-hunt chases through the old woods, clubs formed of boys on one side and girls on the other. We built a shack one year and it was torn down in a triumphant culminating war between the sexes to end the satisfying season.

The vacations always ended suddenly, and where there had been heat and sun, there was the brisk autumn and wind. In the orchard of a nearby farmer, where apples and pears rotted in the grass beneath the trees, I wandered with my net to find the late butterflies, and to augment the insect collection housed in pest-proof boxes.

In the late day my sisters and I looked at stereoscopic photographs. A hundred boxes of them lined one wall; our father had once sold the views for Underwood and Underwood when a young man. It was an unhurried occupation; I put the double picture in the stereograph holder, propped my elbows on the table, and stayed lost in a three-dimensional view of Egypt or Africa until I knew it by heart. We even had a few that had been taken of the family: our father's Irish setters leaping for a stick held high in his hand; our mother with a collie beside her; or myself and Janet with the dogs lined up in a row for the picture-taker, Jack and Benaboy leaning into my knees.

My favorite box was labeled WILD ANIMALS. "Let me show you this one!" I shouted as we sat about the table, each with a viewer held to his eyes.

"Okay, but don't mix them up," my elder sister said.

"I know."

Our father looked in on us, half concerned. He was slipping into his mackinaw for the evening walk. The red setters at his heels barked, their toes skidding on the linoleum. "Are they getting finger marks on them?" he asked our mother. He wanted them respected.

"Are you, children?" she asked.

Janet held one up by the edges. "Look how careful, Daddy."

He was whistling as he left, trilling, warbling like a bird; the door slammed firmly. After an hour he was back, his song in the entry as he hung his coat on the hook; it was one of his foolish *little* tunes:

MONEY

Oh mon-ey is the meat in the co-coa-nut, mon-ey is the milk in the jug; when you got lots of mon-ey, you feel ver-y fun-ny, snug as a bug in a rug!

He had been far up the beach, into the wind that whipped, returning with it at his back. There would be no one down there. Sometimes before he left he phoned a friend who lived five miles up the beach and they started out together and met half way, continued to one house or the other and returned then by car, or again on foot. If the wind were low he took a couple of golf clubs and a few balls, and sometimes a daughter to caddy. He dragged great driftwood logs up on the beach, admiring the wild shapes the lake molded them into, sometimes bringing small ones home for the fires. He threw sticks for the dogs who pranced after with devoted eagerness and returned them to his hand.

After supper, bored, beside the fire, I foolishly challenged everyone, including our father, to checkers. A college champ, he'd had a reputation at a firehouse where he'd worked once. He didn't let me win out of kindness; the games were short and I went down to the tune of a series of jumps that had been set up early by his cunning mind. I learned smiling defeat, my heart pounding in anger, sighing, turning to my dog for comfort, sprawling on the floor.

"I still think I can beat you," I stated. "Will you play tomorrow?"

"It's a date, Swipes," he grinned.

My sister had brought out the guitar. "Let's sing."

"It's time I go up to work," he told her, gentle.

"But you're going away tomorrow, Daddy!" Margaret's blue eyes were bright, her manner winning.

"True." He already had his arms about the wood thing, his fingers over the strings.

THE COMPANY SONG

We live in com-pa-ny hou-ses, the com-pa-ny runs the schools, we're wor-king for the com-pa-ny ac-cord-ing to the com-pa-ny's rules, we all drink com-pa-ny wat-er, we all burn com-pa-ny lights, and the com-pa-ny's preach-ers teach us what the com-pa-ny thinks is right!

Years later, I heard of the song's history, of men who never saw regular money, and went to a Company window and drew brass tokens against their accounts, which could only be spent at Company stores.

We sang of a railroad and the unscrupulous fellow who ran it, holding ten thousand miles of track. It was back in the eighties:

ON A MONDAY MORNING

On a Monday morn-ing it be-gan to rain, 'round the bend came a gra-vel train, On the bum-pers was Ho-bo John, He's a good old ho-bo, but he's dead and gone; Dead and gone, dead and gone; he's a good old ho-bo but he's dead and gone!

2

Charley Snyder was a good engineer,
Told his fireman never you fear,
All he needed was water and coal,
Put your head out the window, see the drivers roll,
See the drivers roll, see the drivers roll,
Put your head out the window, see the drivers roll!

3

Jay Gould's daughter says before she died,
"Papa, fix the blind so the bums can't ride,
And if ride they must, let them ride the rod,
Let them put their trust in the hands of God!"
In the hands of God, in the hands of God,
Let them put their trust in the hands of God!"

4

Jay Gould's daughter says before she died,
"There's one more road I'd like to ride."
"Tell me daughter, what can it be?"
"Well, it's the Southern Pacific on the Santa Fe,
On the Santa Fe, on the Santa Fe,
It's the Southern Pacific on the Santa Fe!"

Up on the top of our house was a platform with a railing, benches and a table; it was the "crows nest" and was reached by a staircase slanted against the roof by our country carpenter. The "crows nest" was put there when the Graf Zepplin went by once and we had to clamber up on the hot coarse red shingles of the roof, riding the apex, to watch it pass. In the "crows nest" we sunned in the first hot days of the year, and there we climbed with trays for evening suppers, and in the nights we carried up a secondhand telescope the family had acquired.

We examined the sky for constellations and stars. We called off their names: the Pleiades, Auriga, and the brilliant one, Capella. We watched the slow-motion eclipses of sun and moon and stars, partial and complete.

I learned strange songs with no meaning I could tell. And wandered to my Bible to find prophesying;

> And I looked, and, behold a whirlwind came out of the north, a great cloud, and a fire infolding itself . . . out of the midst thereof came the likeness of four living creatures . . . and they four had one likeness: and their appearance and their work was as it were a wheel in the middle of a wheel . . . . Withersoever the spirit was to go, they went, thither was their spirit to go; . . . and when they went, I heard the noise of their wings, like the noise of great waters, as the voice of the Almighty, the voice of speech, as the noise of an host: when they stood, they let down their wings. And there was a voice from the firmament that was over their heads.

The song went:

EZEKIEL SAW THE WHEEL

E - ze-kiel saw the wheel, E - ze-kiel saw the wheel, way up in the
mid - dle of the air, the big wheel move by faith, and the lit - tle wheel move by the
grace of God; a wheel and a wheel, way up in the mid - dle of the air!

The words were words men had puzzled upon, and offered explanations about, and made the song for; with the arrogance of adolescence, I thought I understood in the way I did the man of the home when he read his poems at the supper table, playing with words:

> . . . *And a monkey picked stars and put them in his mouth, tall up*
> *a tree of stars shining in a south sky panel.*
> *I saw this and I saw when it meant and what it means was five, six,*
> *seven, five, six, seven. . . .*

Down inside the walls of the house, lamp-lit, in the late evenings, there were mournful-sounding tunes, one about a great slave:

NICODEMUS

Ni - co - de - mus the slave, was of A - fri - can birth, he was bought for a bag - ful of gold;
He was re - ckoned as part of the salt of the earth and he died years a - go ve - ry old.
'Twas his last sad re - quest as they laid him a - way In the trunk of an old hol - low tree, "Wake me up," was his charge, "at the first break of day! Wake me up for the great Ju - bi - lee." There's a good time a - com - ing it's al - most here, Been long long long on the way, Go run and tell E - li - jah to hur - ry up come, meet us at the gum tree down in the swamp, To wake Ni - co - de - mus to - day!

2

Nicodemus was never the sport of the lash
Though the bullet had oft crossed his path,
There were none of his masters so brave or so rash
As to face such a man in his wrath;
Yet his great heart was filled with kindness to the brim,
He obeyed who was born to command;
But he longed for the morning which then was so dim,
For the morning which now is at hand.
CHORUS

And then, after a while, as the moon outside slowly spun up high, the head of the house stood up from his chair. "I've got to go to work." And he mounted the staircases that led to the attic. When he was gone, we lingered on the floor or settled in deep chairs, arms about

63

dogs, a cat near by. There were idle songs that were roared at summer camps from one end of the nation to the other every year:

FORTY-NINE BOTTLES

Forty nine bottles hanging on the wall, forty nine bottles hanging on the wall, take one a-way from them all, forty eight bottles hanging on the wall!

2
Forty-eight bottles hanging on the wall,
Forty-eight bottles hanging on the wall,
Take one away from them all,
Forty-seven bottles hanging on the wall!

And so it went. And there were parodies and silly verses we learned from summer resort children:

OLD NOAH

Old No-ah built him-self an ark, the good old Chris-tian soul, he put his fam-i-ly on the deck and the an-i-mals in the hold. go to hell now, go to hell now, go to hell with your damned old lea-ky scow, for it ain't gon-na rain an-y how, an-y how, it ain't gon-na rain an-y how!

2
And as he sailed away from shore
With all his kith and kin,
The neighbors gathered on the bank
And they merrily mocked at him.

3

For forty days and forty nights,
The rain came down like hell,
It covered everything in sight
Including hill and dell.

4

Old Noah walked upon the deck
And looked through a windowpane,
He says, "Where are those goddamn fools
Who said it wasn't gonna rain?"

These were impious harmless ditties. We had one of our own; we felt
the daring, and remembered to quote to each other a saying we knew:
even God gets tired of too much halleluia.

JESUS CHRIST AND ST. PETER

Je-sus Christ and St. Pe-ter went out for a walk, way out on the Sea of Ga-li-lee; said Je-sus to Pe-ter, "Now don't it beat hell, the way that I walk on the sea?

2

St. Peter then answered the Lord Jesus Christ,
Familiarly known as J.C.,
"You have two bladders stuck one on each foot,
No wonder you walk on the sea!"

Sacred tunes were always satirized; many came to us by way of
the Salvation Army:

LOVER OF THE LORD

Oh you must be a lo-ver of the Lord, or you won't get to hea-ven when you die; oh you must be a lov-er of the land-la-dy's daugh-ter or you won't get a piece of pie!

And the white gospel hymn "Showers of Blessings" became

SHOWERS OF DOLLARS

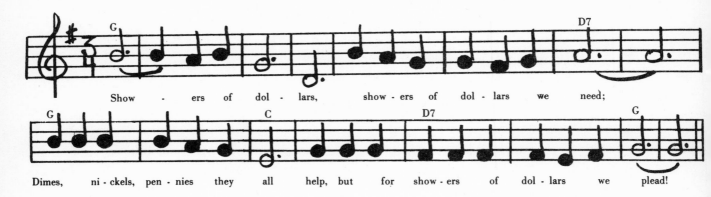

Show - ers of dol - lars, show - ers of dol - lars we need;

Dimes, ni - ckels, pen - nies they all help, but for show - ers of dol - lars we plead!

One of our favorites of the slightly licentious variety had a thousand versions as it traveled up and down the sea, over the railroads, through the schools, into the factories; some versions were ancient, others half a century old, others born yesterday:

GEORGIA STREET HOTEL

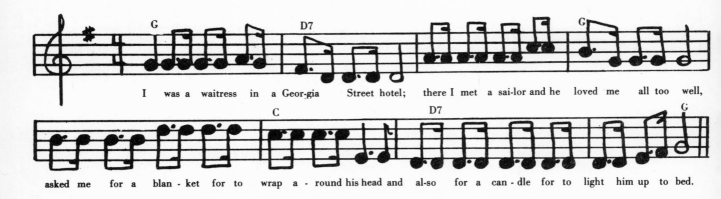

I was a waitress in a Geor-gia Street hotel; there I met a sai-lor and he loved me all too well,

asked me for a blan - ket for to wrap a - round his head and al-so for a can - dle for to light him up to bed.

2

I being single, thought 'twould do no harm
To jump into bed for to keep a sailor warm,
That was the start of all my misery;
Never trust a man who sails upon the sea!

3

Early in the morning, before the break of day,
A dollar bill he handed me, and then these words did say,
"You might have a daughter and you might have a son,
But take this, little darling, for the damage I have done!

4

"Now, if it be a daughter, bounce her on your knee,
And if it be a son, send the bastard out to sea
In bell bottom trousers of a wicked wicked hue,
Make him climb the rigging like his daddy used to do."

5

The moral of this story is plain as it can be,
Never trust a sailor-boy an inch above your knee;
I trusted one and look what he done,
Ran away and left me with a good-for-nothing son!

And there was a silly ballad, not so gray-haired, which we rendered in the summertime from the stage of our amateur theater, which was one end of the main room of some bare-floored summer cottage. The audience was ordinarily smaller than the cast. A girl, dressed in her brother's clothes, put on a top hat and lowered her voice:

THE MAN WHO COMES AROUND

There's a man who comes to our house, ev-ry sin-gle day; Pa-pa comes home and the man goes a-way; Pa-pa does the work and Ma-ma gets the pay, and a man comes a-round when Pa-pa goes a-way!

2

There's a man who comes to our house, comes to take the trash;
He's tall and dark and got a cute mustache;
Now, I'm not saying nothing but it seems to me
He's just a little nicer than a trashman ought to be.

3

There's a man who comes to our house, comes to bring the milk;
He's tall and dark and smooth as silk;
I have to watch his horse tied down by the gate,
Because he stays so long that the horse don't want to wait.

4

There's a man who comes to our house, comes to bring the ice;
He's tall and dark and he's so very nice;
But the little piece of ice melts so very fast away,
He's got to come back a little later in the day.

5

Well, when I grow up I don't want to be
A doctor or a lawyer or the head of a family;
I don't want to be a butcher or a baker down town,
I just want to be the man who comes around!

The family liked a few popular songs, and when one was elected it was added to the store. One was pensive, "The Isle of Capri." We kept it along with other songs, humming them after most of the nation had forgot:

> Pack up all my care and woe
> Here I go singing low, Bye bye, Blackbird!

Sometimes, across the lake, a mystery would appear. Opening the door and going down to the beach for a walk before bed, we saw above the place where Chicago was, the lights of a building, and sometimes its shape. The mirage would not stay for long. Chicago was far away and strange; there I had gone for haircuts with my sister, in a strange and wonderful barbershop in Marshall Field's; and there we had been taken for gymnastic lessons for a little time.

We had always heard jokes told of it, familiarly, by friends who came from there, by our father who had made it his own. He told sometimes of Jesus and two men walking down Clark Street and stopping in at a dice game. Jesus rolled a seven on his first throw out of the box; next came an eleven. He was preparing to shake the dice again. "Come on," someone objected, "let's play craps. None of your high-falutin' miracles."

All of growing up was a mystery. We had heard about death, and one day it was our own grandmother, Oma. I met the knowledge uncertain; unhappy, unused to the emotion, I walked down by the lake, sulking. There were adult burdens to shoulder slowly.

In a novel later I recited the strangeness of adolescence, the slow half-willing assumption of pain and responsibility:

> About them the fog draped the woods ghostly, changing its character, hiding what stood behind, and making what stood before seem to come forward, larger, a little ominous. Boles of trees that had reared stark and black in the winter months, now in the Eden of May, covered their parts with young green; vague, they were wreathed in the mist.
>
> The children stood there in the woods with the mare and the hands of time stopped for a while. It was the sort of moment that would come back in dreams the rest of their lives, like a comfort. The three were reunited, and for the moment had no connection with the rest of the world. Tomorrow the girl's father, an outlander, might wield the power of an adult and take the mare away. And Men of Law might again lead the boy back to his foster home with his uncle. The girl might be lonely and hurt. But that was the future, another hour. Now she was patting Blueberry at the same moment that the boy was. They recognized what was happening and stood quiet. Then they felt the handles creak and time again turned.

Children's ways are unimpeded. In another book, the brother and sister are in the summer house on a Sunday evening. The boy has his white rat, Davy, on the bed with him, for Davy was a pet rat that I had loved dearly; it is curled on the pillow by his ear. His sister, named for my paternal Grandmother Sandburg, has come to stand beside him, overcome by her welling of feeling. Gus, who was named after Grandfather Sandburg, invites her to have a chair:

> "Thanks." Clara pushed his tennis shoes off onto the sandy floor, and sat, her elbows on her knees, her hands hanging listless. It was almost seven

o'clock. Clara thought of how she'd used to tap her foot three times, or dive under seven times; how numbers had meant special colors. She was breaking herself of the train of thought, and would deliberately mix everything up, using fours and nines, warring doggedly with her other nature. She had all sorts of new disciplines she contrived. One was to exercise, push-ups and waist-bends, till she thought she'd drop. Another was making lists of what to do for every hour of the day to improve herself. She felt she was on the verge of becoming perfect. There was only one thing that she'd have traded for being just what she was; that was to be a Catholic novice nun, who could kneel on a bare rough cold brick floor with arms spread wide all through a dark empty night and fall exhausted in a dead faint at sunrise before an enormous bloodied crucifix of some perfectly tremendous wooden god. What she wouldn't give, she thought.

"What are you doing, Gus?" she asked her brother.

"Nothing. Just lying, thinking." He put a slender finger to touch his white rat's head and back.

"Why?"

They said nothing for a while. Their life was a wheel that turned round and round over the days, and there seemed no end or beginning of it. They remained the same age forever; they were unable to conceive of themselves as adults some day. "I'll be glad when I'm grown up," said Gus, not believing it would happen, not in his presumable future. "I'll live by myself in a one-room stone house."

"What about your wife?"

"I'm not going to marry. If I do it'll be when I'm old; about forty."

Mum called from below. The children sat as though the voice hadn't reached them; they didn't stir. Mum gave them up and the screen slapped downstairs after her.

"Let's go," Gus said and got up to take Davy by his neck scruff to his cage and close the lid.

Clara led the way. The shell of the old house was empty except for the pair descending the creaky front stairs. They each felt a quick unnamed edge of an unknown fear; might someone be skulking behind the faded striped drapes that hung nearly to the floor beside the windows where the dusk moved? They hid their alarm, each from the other, their steps swift as they went out the door.

When we had lived in the duneland country for a few years we became earth-hungry, and acquired a little acreage in back of Pawpaw Patch and named it a farm. Again our mother was drawing blueprints, this time outlining where the rows of grapes would stand, where the bush fruit, where the strawberry bed. There were x's to mark a tiny orchard of plums, pears, apricots, peaches, nectarines, apples, cherries.

And then it blossomed like a fairy tale in the greening spring, the white of cherry, the pink of apple and peach blows. We stared at the miracle, our hands, the fingernails rimmed with dirt, upon the handles of the hand plow which marked the garden rows, and had a detachable blade, later fitted with a cultivator head to guide up and down the wavering lines of varied shades and shapes of green: spikey onion sets, scrolled lettuce, dark spinach. We stood over them in the half-fog, half-rain, damp seed packets in our coat pockets; we spent evenings hanging over the catalogs, humming. Sometimes the tune had bars missing, but it was the way we'd learned it and it sounded good, melancholy; and it held solace:

BENDERMERE STREAM

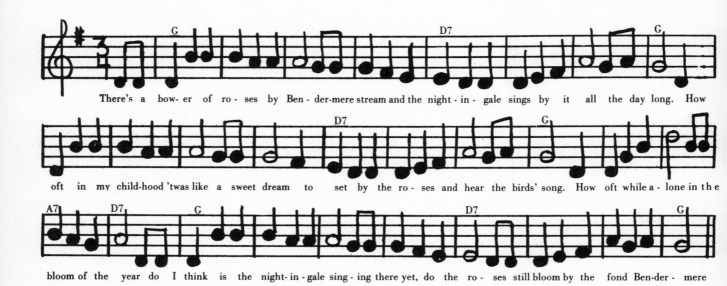

There's a bow-er of ro-ses by Ben-der-mere stream and the night-in-gale sings by it all the day long. How oft in my child-hood 'twas like a sweet dream to set by the ro-ses and hear the birds' song. How oft while a-lone in the bloom of the year do I think is the night-in-gale sing-ing there yet, do the ro-ses still bloom by the fond Ben-der-mere

When our mother stood beside the hired man, out on the new land, he was helpless before her power, her small capable broad hands. She declared, "No. That hole's too small."

"But there's a-plenty room, now," he argued, towering huge above her little shape.

"It's got to be bigger."

She leaned to lift the great soil-ball encased in sacking that surrounded the roots of the dwarf apple tree. She set it next to her and with the shovel enlarged the hole to suit her feeling. The small tree was replaced and the nails pulled out that held the sacking. Then the roots were spread with care, the soil tamped firmly. She left the man to fill the water-cave about the tree from bucket or hose, while she went to get another seedling from those waiting, heeled in with soil to keep them alive.

I turned back to the tiny plow, already planning to suggest additions to the farm. I wanted living things that moved more swiftly than trees: I wanted hens and ducks, and if our parents could be convinced, a cow. I sang in the spring mist, a lusty song, patriotic, written by one of our soldier-patriots, Joseph Warren, before he fell at the Battle of Breed's Hill back a hundred and fifty years:

FREE AMERIKAY

That seat of sci-ence, A-thens, and earth's proud mis-tress, Rome, Where now are all their glo-ries? You scarce can find a tomb! Then guard your rights, A-mer-i-cans, Nor stoop to law-less sway, Op-pose, op-pose, op-pose! for free A-mer-i-kay!

2

Torn from a world of tyrants
Beneath this western sky,
We formed a new dominion,
A land of liberty;
The world shall own we're masters here,
Then hasten on the day,
Huzza, huzza, huzza! for free Amerikay!

3

God bless this maiden climate,
And through its vast domain
May hosts of heroes cluster
Who scorn to wear a chain,
And blast the venal sycophant
That dares our rights betray,
Huzza, huzza, huzza! for free Amerikay.

4

Lift up your hands, ye heroes,
And swear with proud disdain,
The wretch that would ensnare you
Shall lay his snares in vain,
Should Europe empty all her force
We'll meet her in array,
And fight and shout and fight! for North Amerikay.

5

Some future day shall crown us
The masters of the main,
Our fleets shall speak in thunder
To England, France, and Spain,
And the nations over the ocean
Shall tremble and obey
The sons, the sons, the sons of brave Amerikay!

There were all sorts of outdoor songs to sing, while one leaned over gardens or tramped up and down sand hills, placing the feet in tracks of the one who went before. There were the songs of shootings and deaths:

BRADY

Dun-can and his bro-ther was play-ing pool, In came Bra-dy act-ing the fool,
Dun-can shot him once, he shot him twice, Says, "I don't make my liv-ing by shoot-ing dice."

CHORUS

Bra - dy, why di - dn't you run? Bra - dy, you should of run;
Bra - dy, why di - dn't you run? When you seen Black Dun-can with his gat - ling gun!

2

"Brady, Brady, don't you know you done wrong
To come in my house when the game was going on?
I told you half a dozen times before,
Now you're lying dead on my barroom floor."

3

Brady went to hell, looking mighty curious,
Devil says, "Where you from?" "East St. Louis."
"Well, pull off your coat and step this-a-way,
'Cause I've been expecting you every day!"

4

When the girls heard that Brady was dead
They went up home and they put on red;
They came down town singing this song:
"Brady's strutting in hell with his Stetson on!

CHORUS

"Brady, where you at?
Brady, where you at?
Brady, where you at?
Brady's strutting in hell in his Stetson hat!"

And the one about violation of the commandments against adultery and murder, and the resultant crime, grieving, and punishment. It had been jazzed and blued and wailed and sung serious, all about the nation, back in the mountains, along the big rivers, over to San Francisco, up in the Dakotas. The heroine was variously called Josie, Sadie, or Lillie; the villain, Albert the gambler, or Henry Brown.

Typical of the ballad, handed down and pieced together, it blandly ignored the switch from electric chair to gallows:

FRANKIE AND JOHNNY

Fran - kie and John - ny were lov - ers, Oh Lor- dy, how they could love, Swore to be true to each oth - er, True as the stars a - bove; he was her ma - n, but he done her wrong!

2

Frankie and Johnny went walking,
Johnny in his brand new suit;
"Oh good Lord," Says Frankie,
"Don't my Johnny look cute!"
He was her man, who was doing her wrong!

3

Frankie went down to the corner
To buy herself a cool glass of beer;
Says, "Tell me, Mr. Bartender,
Has my lovingest man been here?
He is my man, and he's doing me wrong."

4

"I don't want to tell you no stories,
I don't want to tell you no lies,
I seen your man about an hour ago
With a gal called Allie Bly;
He is your man, but he's doing you wrong."

5

Frankie went down to the pawnshop,
Bought herself a little forty-four,
Aimed it at the ceiling,
Shot a big hole in the floor.
"Where is my man, what's doing me wrong?"

6

Frankie went down to the hotel,
She rang that hotel bell;
"Stand back all you floozies
Or I'll blow you all to hell!
I want my man, what's doing me wrong!"

7

Frankie went up the stairway,
She looked in the transom so high,
There she saw her loving Johnny,
Loving up Allie Bly;
He was her man, but he was doing her wrong.

8

Frankie threw back her kimono,
She took out her little forty-four;
Roota-toot-toot, three times she shot
Right through that hardwood door;
Shot her man, what done her wrong.

9

Johnny grabbed off his Stetson,
"Good Lord, Frankie, don't shoot!"
But she put her finger on the trigger
And the gun went *roota-toot-toot*;
He was her man, and she shot him down.

10

"Oh my baby, kiss me
Once before I go,
Roll me over on my right side
So the bullet don't hurt me so;
I was her man, but I done her wrong!"

11

"Bring out your long black coffin,
Bring out your rubber-tired hack,
They're taking Johnny to the burying-ground
And they won't bring a bit of him back,
He was my man, but he done me wrong."

12

Frankie says to the warden,
"Warden, what they gonna do?"
The warden says to Frankie,
"It's the electric chair for you,
You shot your man when he done you wrong."

13

The judge says to the jury,
"It's plain as plain can be,
This woman shot her lover
And it's murder in the second degree,
He was her man and he done her wrong."

14

Now it wasn't murder in the second degree
And it wasn't murder in the third,
The woman simply dropped her man
The way a hunter drops a bird;
He was her man, but he done her wrong.

15
Frankie mounted the scaffold,
Calm as a girl could be;
Turning her eyes up to heaven she says,
"Nearer my God to thee!
He was my man, but he done me wrong!"

16
Frankie sit in the parlor,
Cool herself with a 'lectric fan,
Telling all the other women and girls,
"Never trust no gambling man,
He'll be your man, but he'll do you wrong!"

And my proposal to add laying hens to the farm was met with the suggestion that we have ducks too. My desire for geese was augmented by others' desire for pigs, and we got two from a farmer. Soon we had all but the cow. Our father said it would never fit in with the miniature character of the place.

"Get a milk goat."

"He's right," we said, pleased. And promptly, my mother and I journeyed about the countryside, escaping butting by a number of horned and smelly, squat and strange creatures, until at last we came to a farm where the Swiss breeds of dairy goats were kept.

We made a deal and five animals stepped into the back of the car where the seat had been removed and straw put down. They were crossbreds and handsome: Leona, white and horned and gracious; Meggi, reddish; Sophie, brown and smooth; and her doeling Mazli; and Mazli's nursing kid, Heidi.

In days to pass we returned to the farmer and acquired a purebred he consented to sell, Felicia, chocolate and affectionate. We called our place the Tom Thumb Dairy, and then as we got into the breeding of purebred goats, named it, ambitious, the Chikaming Goat Farm. We nailed up a sign and printed the name on our stationery. We raised Toggenburg, Saanen, and Nubian milk goats.

We bought baby chicks and ducklings and goslings, who paraded about making soft pleading sounds. I gave them crumbled hard-boiled eggs with some wet chick mash, hovering over them.

In some way, in the next year, I convinced everyone of the economy and wisdom of my ownership of a mare. She was to eat the leftovers from the goats' feed—the hay they refused—and she was to work about the place, carrying sacks of hay on her back to the buck quarters that stood up on the dune above the farm. She came before long, a buckskin called Nancy. She loved to swim in the lake and to explore the country. I adored her and later wrote a book in her celebration.

Both of us being balky but obliging of nature, Nancy and I got on. Soon she would kneel and lie down and rear up for me. She learned by a method I had read of in a series of pamphlets sold to me by a country school friend. He had used the method with success on horses he knew at a stable. Being the child of poor parents, the oldest of a great number of siblings, he wanted money. Originally he bought the set through the mail. A series of letters had come, first offering them for fifty dollars and then forty and down the line, until my tense friend had paid fifteen dollars. I gave him ten.

Once I visited his home while we were out riding, and his mother asked me to stay for lunch. We waited while the younger children finished their meal, eaten standing about a newspaper-covered table, and consisting of crackers and peanut butter and jam and milk. My mouth watered. Polite, I waited to eat in splendor at a cloth-covered table, from the meat meant for their supper.

Nancy and I were inseparable. One cold February, using one of my new skills, I helped deliver the twins of a goat on a cold morning, I wrapped them in burlap, got on the mare and cantered to our house in the distance, where there was a warm kitchen. It was one of the family's Western songs:

THE COLORADO TRAIL

Eyes like the morning star, Cheeks like a rose, Laury was a pretty girl God almighty knows; Weep, all you bitter rains, Wail, wind, wail, All along, along, along the Colorado Trail!

The farm was a great affair in the lives of the family. When we had first got the ducks and one had laid an egg, the flag was hoisted on the pole that stood on the high dune behind our house. Then I ate the egg for breakfast. When the speckled pullet had left an egg in one of the wood nest boxes made by our hired man, there was a similar fete.

I had taken typing in high school and was beginning to help the author in the house, sometimes with correspondence, sometimes copying marked passages in books and papers, and typing from manuscripts, often in his special shorthand; and again taking dictation. I climbed up to his workroom at the top of the stairway in the attic. There was a homey shack-like feel to his rooms, as if a pot of coffee were close at hand. My fingers rested on the typewriter keys waiting for the next word.

"Stick around, Swipes," he promised, "and we'll open a keg of nails."

"Okay."

And after an hour of work he leaned back and straightened his shoulders. He cut a cigar expertly in half with a small steel pocket-knife. "Follow me and you'll wear diamonds." He grinned.

"Hey. Swell."

There were bookshelves and orange crates; his typewriter stood on one and a paper supply on the shelf inside. He nodded at me, his blue-green eyes on fire. He began composing aloud again, and my machine rattled. It was late in the hours when I finally left. The cigar in his teeth was out. He looked up tender, "Don't be afraid of loneliness, Swipes."

"I know what you mean," I swore, "and I'm not afraid to die either."

I had felt my danger sometimes when I rode Nancy in the black of night down upon the soft sand of the beach shore, or when we swam out too far, or when I let her race. I jumped her over barriers high and higher, raising the logs, testing her. She was clever and willing. Often I was cast from her, clutching the reins, and sometimes felt the shock of it. And so I said to him and later put it in a book, "If I get killed riding my mare I just want you to know that I've died happy!" I felt I'd tasted experience to the brim.

Mild, he let me go. The flue for his small wood stove coiled up into the ceiling; there was a box of dry twisted paper and kindling in a corner, driftwood that he'd brought in from his walks on the shore. There was an open sink where he washed and shaved, Indian blankets and ponchos on the floor and covering his spare bed which stood beside his work. There were big army metal record cans about.

I went down the stairs two at a time; I heard him humming a little bittersweet song.

PAPA LOVED MAMA

Pa - pa loved Ma - ma, Ma - ma loved men, Ma - ma's in the grave - yard, Pa - pa's in the pen!

He had other tiny bittersweet songs.

GREAT GOD, I'M FEELING BAD

Great God, I'm feel - ing bad, I ain't got the man that I thought I had!

In later years I made a poem for our father, and showed it to my sister and mother, read it for a few friends, shy; not to him.

ADDRESSED TO A FATHER

I remember you in various ways;
The picture I have of you of those days
Differs perhaps from what you'd think it is.
Living is an unprobed game that children play
Since everyone else is doing it too.

You sat on the house's top above three stairways,
Your skin caging the sun with brassed felicity,
And spoke to me father's counsel
To which I gave little mind,
Though admiring your glad attitude, and being
Sure that the world was firm, since you held
Its reins so exceeding well. The smoke
Had gone from your cold clenched cigar; the wood
Of the orange crate was hot to touch; in back
Of you the iron grill was flooded by a trumpet vine;
The tropical blooms hid clustering from
The sun which was stamped with your name,
Which belonged I knew to you.

That was one thing, the sun; another was
Your voice humming as you descended uncounted stairs
To where the rest of us were at table.
Two mad beautiful Irish setters howling joy
Prefaced your arrival. A song had begun lusty
When you reached the second staircase; it might be,

The faces in the room went wheeling to your voice. Then
Your affection for night, your walking through it,
Into its blackness where occasionally glowed
One evening star like a tiny sun
Or the beginning moon like a cobweb looped
Or an old sated one in the blue blaze.

For these thanks: the globe and bugle blooms, the red dogs
And song, the night which I hold on temporary loan.

As the produce came from the farm we canned and preserved. In the proper season dozens of quarts of peaches glistened on the counters in the gold afternoon sunlight. And when tomatoes were in season, we stayed in the kitchen long after sunset. The floor was gritty and a few of the red globes still remained in the grimy baskets. The door stood open and the sweet wind swept through the house. The dogs came in, reeking of a skunk they had run down. They were ordered outside and lay on the brick walk in the path of light that streamed from the kitchen.

The farm became a serious affair, and I spent more and more time at it. I put aside the ways of adolescence and stopped playing so much; I bent myself, a natural farmer, to the land and the beasts, my emotion for them sturdy and maternal. Because I rose at a pre-dawn hour, I typed mainly in daylight hours. I carried a machine out to the barn and in a loft room, the animals moving and munching in the straw down below, I copied whatever was turned over to me by our father, and began keeping records too, and correspondence on the farm and the goat herd.

The scent up there of new-cut alfalfa hay was affecting, there being a satisfaction to its particular sweetness. I had first breathed it in Thomas Hardy's country novels, in certain of Chekhov's works, and Ibsen's. It resembled the odor of a suckling puppy or a well-kept stable, perhaps.

Nancy stamped down below me, impatient. There were other horses who came and went, mounts for my sisters and friends. There was Nip and the blue roan Denny, and Kentucky, and a headstrong heavy gray called Silver who, once she learned to stand on her hind legs, stood squarely like a magnificent fabled creature.

And in the late afternoons before milking time, I put on my swim suit and went to lead Nancy from the barn. She knelt and I went bareback over the dune to the beach to swim in the blue. In half an hour we were galloping back. Later, when the last of the day was spending itself, and the milking was over, the eggs collected, the final feeding done, the family went for a walk on the yet warm beach sand.

There the sunset was going through its long slow garish explosion above Chicago across the water. We whispered because of the cathedral-like atmosphere of the coming twilight. The wind blew a little and all the dunes moved a fragment one way or another. The shore darkened; we wound our path up the sand mounds, and through the woods, and down the winding road home.

With slow steps each found his corner of the house, our parents to their desks, Margaret to her piano or books, Janet and myself to bed. The whippoorwill started its calling as I drowsed into sleep.

In the morning I crept down at still-dark, four o'clock. Voices rose and fell from the dining room, where the two still sat. Among the dishes and silver, the glasses and linen, would be the bread-dough dice our father had worked as he talked, marking in the numbers with fork-prongs. Our mother's hands would be fingering a goat pedigree or some sweater she mended as their talk wandered on politics and convictions.

I tiptoed past them into the cool scented night, a book under my arm. The old moon was falling and spreading its whiteness on the path; shadows were faint. I turned my back on the house's square of window light that shone on the pine trees and headed for the looming darkened barns. In the pungent odor there, I snapped on the lights and clattered the milk pails, and spoke to the animals. While milking I memorized the poets, the book propped on the stand beside me; the white foam flowed over the pail-sides. William Blake and Sara Teasdale, Elizabeth or Robert Browning:

> *"Dust and ashes!" So you creak it,*
> *And I want the heart to scold.*
> *Dear dead women, with such hair, too—*
> *What's become of all the gold*
> *Used to hang and brush their bosoms?*
> *I feel chilly and grown old.*

There were others, Lord Tennyson:

> *Break, break, break,*
> *On thy cold gray stones, O Sea!*
> *And I would that my tongue could utter*
> *The thoughts that arise in me!*
>
> *Break, break, break,*
> *At the foot of thy crags, O Sea!*
> *But the tender grace of a day that is dead*
> *Will never come back to me.*

I felt my life was going by too swiftly. Returning the milker to her stall, I got another.

I turned on the barn radio. The singers at that hour directed themselves to farmers like myself. They made remarks about us. One professional rube told of the ventriloquist who had the cows chiding the hired man, "Why don't you warm up your cold hands, mister!"

I joined in the melodies with vigor:

NOBODY'S DARLING

You're as pure as the flow-ers in spring - time, You're as sweet as the dew on the rose, I would ra - ther be some - bo - dy's dar - ling, than a poor boy that no-bo- dy knows!

The does brought up their cuds with small wheezes, and chewed and swallowed, placid. They were not startled by bursts of melody from the little box, or by the twang and beat of that hour's brand of

entertainers: the words were all alike; I sang them incorrectly, but it
never mattered:

> Sweethearts or strangers, it makes no difference now,
> I leave it up to you!
> Sweethearts or strangers, I'll get along somehow;
> What am I going to do?

There at the milk stand I first heard Woody Guthrie:

JESUS CHRIST

Je - sus Christ was a man that trav-eled thru the land, A car - pen - ter true and brave, Says to the rich, "Give your goods to the poor," And they laid Je - sus Christ in His grave. Je - sus was a man, a car - pen - ter by hand, a car - pen - ter true and brave, and a dir - ty lit - tle cow-ard called Ju - das Is - car - i - at Laid Je - sus Christ in His grave.

2

He went to the sick and He went to the poor,
He went to the hungry and the lame,
Says that the poor would one day win the world,
And so they laid Jesus Christ in his grave.

3

They nailed Him there to die on a cross in the sky
In the lightning and the thunder and the rain,
And Judas Iscariot committed suicide
When they laid poor Jesus in his grave.

4

When the love of the poor shall some day turn to hate,
And the patience of the workers gives away,
'Twould be better for you rich if you never had of been born
For you laid Jesus Christ in his grave!

Morning after morning I listened, over WLS to the "Smile-a-while" program:

DEAR EVALINA

Like a rose she is fair, Like a lamb she is meek, and she's ne- ver been known to put paint on her cheek, In - to long grace-ful curls falls her ra- ven black hair And she nev- er re- quires per- fu - mer - y there! Dear Ev- a - li- na, my sweet Ev- a - li- na, my love for thee shall ne- ver ne- ver die; Dear Ev- a - li- na, my sweet Ev- a - li- na, my love for thee shall never, ne- ver die!

I heard religious tunes, gospel hymns, accompanying the singer at the top of my voice. When it neared six o'clock the hired hand was due to arrive. He formed the habit of slamming the door as he entered, so I recognized his presence, and lowered my voice.

It was Jeremiah, Chapter 12, verse 9:

Mine heritage is unto me as a speckled bird, the birds round about are against her:

THE GREAT SPECKLED BIRD

What a beau-ti- ful thought I am think - ing, con - cer - ning the great speck - led bird, re- mem- ber her name is re - cor - ded, on the pa - ges of God's ho - ly word!

2

All the other birds flocking around her,
And she is despised by the squad,
But the great speckled bird in the Bible
Is one with the great church of God.

3

She is spreading her wings for a journey,
She is going to leave by and by,
When the trumpet shall sound in the morning
She will rise and go up in the sky.

4

In the presence of all her despisers,
With a song never uttered before,
She will rise and be gone in a moment
Till the great tribulation is o'er.

5

When He cometh descending from Heaven
On the cloud, as is wrote in the Word,
I'll be joyfully carried up to meet Him
On the wings of the great speckled bird!

Our mother had become an expert on bloodlines and was clever at pedigrees. She and I were especially devoted to the dairy herd. I followed her orders on the chart listing which doe was to be bred by which buck. She knew why. When the kids arrived we gave them a yard of their own and inside Lilliputian quarters with hay racks and keyhole stanchions. Outside we set up a teeter-totter for them and tar barrels for them to roll. They lined up to use their toys, became adept at balancing. They chewed their cuds as they played quietly in their droll fashion. Then one, snorting, would start a gay dash round and round the yard, to end on the teeter-totter or up on a barrel, breathing heavily, motionless again.

Our herd began making milk production records here and there, and we were selling top-quality kids. We brought in sires from the best herds in the country to improve the bloodlines. We started attending state fairs regularly, bringing our exhibits.

We went to Illinois State Fair and there won the Governor Horner's trophy for Best Eight Head in our first year. We had contracted "show fever." We found a secondhand trailer, and made removable partitions to fit inside. We bedded it with straw and transported the show stock in it. At three in the morning, by moonlight, we drove off, arriving in the next afternoon. We led the animals into the stalls provided for them by the state. We swept out the straw from the trailer, cleaned it up, and lived there. We slept in it at night, cooked a little, read sometimes during the day when the animals in their pens were cared for and content.

Sometimes it was blazing hot and exhibitors had to wet down the aisles to settle the dust, and set up fans over the stalls. Even then the animals, clipped and brushed, were often brought panting into the show rings. Now and then it poured rain; storms blew and thunder cracked. Sometimes on the way to the fairgrounds we were delayed by some accident to the trailer or car which had to be repaired; once I was ticketed for going through a stop.

Then at last, at the fair, with offspring of other breeders of dairy goats or cattle, hogs, sheep, squabs, rabbits, we wandered about. We put on flowered dresses with swing skirts, and big hats and high heels and were escorted to the rodeo or the horse show. And in fresh-pressed white jodhpurs and shirt, we went to see the concessions and the side shows, to ride the Ferris wheel, to watch the judging of whatever was going on. We listened to the tinkle of music from the coffee and barbecue cafés and ice cream concessions:

THE OLD PINE TREE

Oh, they cut down the old pine tree, And they hauled it a-way to the mill, to make a cof-fin of pine for that sweet-heart of mine; Oh, they cut down the old pine tree! She's lone-some now in her grave to-nite and there my heart will ev-er be, tho we drift-ed a-part, still they cut down my heart when they cut down the old pine tree!

2
She's lonesome now in her grave tonight,
And there my heart will ever be,
Though we drifted apart, still they cut down my heart
When they cut down the old pine tree!

And then we broke a couple of fresh bales of straw and bedded the trailer again, loaded the stock in and came home. Again we drove during the night so that the stock would keep cool and would sleep. I was singing a poem that had been written by a girl from Red Cloud, Nebraska, with an independent turn of mind and a fresh way of saying things. She wrote movingly of the farmlands and the plows and the people I loved—Willa Cather. The words were set to music by a friend of my father, who taught it to him; and he in turn gave it to his daughters:

SPANISH JOHNNY

The old west, the old time, the old wind sing - ing thru, the

red red grass a thou - sand miles— and Span - ish John - ny you! He'd

sit be - side the wa - ter ditch when all his herd was in, And

ne - er mind a child, but sing to his man - do - lin!

2
The big stars, the blue night, the moon-enchanted plain;
The olive man who never spoke, but sang the songs of Spain.
His speech with men was wicked talk—to hear it was a sin;
But those were golden things he said to his mandolin.

3
The gold songs, the gold stars, the world so golden then;
And the hand so tender to a child had killed so many men.
He died a hard death long ago before the Road came in—
The night before he swung, he sang to his mandolin.

Our father at Umpawaug, the Steichen home in Connecticut, one fall in the late 20's or early 30's.

Our father and my maternal grandfather, Opa, with my oldest sister, Margaret (2 weeks old) in his arms. 1911

Our mother, in the early 1920's. Photograph by her brother, Edward Steichen.

In the back yard of our home in Elmhurst. Janet, age 4, myself, age 2, and Margaret, age 9.

Our father and Uncle Ed,
with Uncle's Irish Wolf-
hound, Fingal.

With my sister,
Janet, age 7, and
our mother's
mother, Oma. Photo-
graph by Oma's son,
Edward Steichen.

In the garden of
our home in Elm-
hurst with Eugene
Debs (who holds a
rose in his hand).
I was 5.

My sister, Janet,
age 7. Photograph
by our uncle,
Edward Steichen.

A photograph of me,
age 5, by our
uncle.

A school photograph of me, age almost 7, on a pony.

Janet, my middle sister, age 8, in the garden of the Elmhurst house, wearing her elf costume.

Our father, his mother, Clara, and me with my dolls, Nell and Betsy, in our garden at Elmhurst.

My sister, Janet (right), and myself
(left) with our father. Elmhurst,
Illinois. Photograph by our uncle.

Our father with Janet, my middle
sister, 12 years old. They are
in front of our dune house at
Harbert. 1928.

Our father with his Irish setters,
Cullie and Dan, at the "point" overlooking Lake Michigan. Harbert, in
the 1930's.

Our home at Harbert, Michigan
which our mother designed and
and had built. The house is
set on top of a sand dune.

The kid yard at Chikaming Goat Farm, Harbert, Michigan. 1938.

Janet (13), myself (11), and the dogs at our Harbert house.

Riding my first mare, Nancy, in Lake Michigan just below our home at Harbert.

At the barndoor, Chikaming Goat Farm, with some of my goats.

On Silver at Harbert. Photograph by my uncle, Edward Steichen.

Listening to our father tell
a fish story while on the
ice floes of Lake Michigan.

Our father and John Carl,
age 3, on a Michigan
beach as a storm comes
up.   1944 or 1945.

"Mr. McGillicuddy"

Our father and Snick, my daughter, in his
attic workroom at Connemara Farm.   1946.

At Connemara Farm with one of
my prize milkers, Brenda. 1948.

Snick, age 5, on her horse,
Remember, age 3. Connemara
Farm.

Our father and my children,
Paula (7) and John Carl (8),
at Connemara Farm.

A photograph which our father
sent to Snick.

Our father with his Washburn guitar
which he later presented to John
Carl.

In the living room of my Washington apartment with the guitar I
bought in Göteborg, Sweden.

My son, John Carl Steichen, age 21,
in Munich, Germany with the Italian
Monzino guitar I sent him from Europe.

Karlen Paula (Snick) with her guitar
(twin to mine) and also bought in
Sweden during my trip there. 1963.

PART THREE

. . . One song leads on to another,
One friend to another friend . . .
—WILFRID W. GIBSON

And I married and went to live and have my babies down the flat country called "Little Egypt" which is across the river from St. Louis, in Illinois. It was a part of the land that the pioneers were singing of on their way to the south of the state, as they went traveling up and down mountains, through Kentucky, over the Ohio River by the Shawneetown ferry, heading for the rich wet land.

We had sung the song in my home, pronouncing the state's name, *Elenoy:*

THE STATE OF ILLINOIS

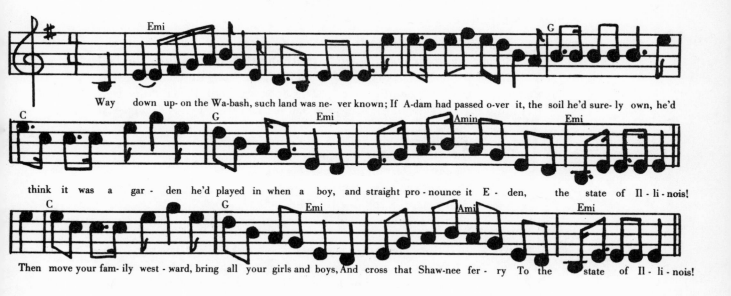

Way down up-on the Wa-bash, such land was ne-ver known; If A-dam had passed o-ver it, the soil he'd sure-ly own, he'd

think it was a gar-den he'd played in when a boy, and straight pro-nounce it E - den, the state of Il-li-nois!

Then move your fam-ily west-ward, bring all your girls and boys, And cross that Shaw-nee fer-ry To the state of Il-li-nois!

2
She's bounded by the Wabash, the Ohio and the Lakes,
She's crawfish in the swampy lands, the milk-sick and the shakes;
But these are slight diversions and take not from the joy
Of living in this garden land, the state of Illinois.

3
'Twas here the Queen of Sheba came with Solomon of old,
With an ass-load of spices, pomegranates and fine gold;
And when she saw this lovely land, her heart was filled with joy,
Straightway she said, "I'd like to be a queen in Illinois!"

89

I took naturally to the farm people, in Michigan, and then in Illinois, and later when we migrated to North Carolina. The house I lived in had two rooms. The outhouse was a few steps from the door. There was a sink in the kitchen which had a drain, but no running water. One went out to the sweet-water well during the day and filled the bucket in which a dipper stood. Everyone dipped and drank; it was the custom in many of the farmer's houses, ignoring fetishes about germs and the like. On a wood table I made Oma's bread, using her Rule For Three Loaves. No spoons or tools were employed, and it was done with the hands:

Dissolve the yeast cake with a bit of sugar in a small dish of warm water, and leave till it bubbles; give it ten minutes or so according. Put six cups flour in a bowl and a handful of salt. Now three cups water, maybe a quart. Warm (hot water makes lumpy flour). Then almost a teacup of melted lard or butter or bacon fat. Then the yeast, now working. Each time you add, mix with fingers, till it gets soupy. Now the rest of the flour (12 cups total, according to water), and dump out on board and work till it squeaks good. Let it raise. Push it down once. Make three loaves up and brush with water for a crust. Bake about an hour.

When I wrote my first book, I told about that life and those people and the songs they sang, the way they spoke and the animals they owned and the crops they made. I told of their household customs that I had watched and engaged in, of their bees and flowers. And their songs. One passage goes:

In the kitchen she was placing the sadirons on the stove to heat. She brought out the ironing board, patched with bleached feed sacking, and laid it crosswise on the end of the table. She spit on the irons to test them, went about her work with familiar hands. The floor was cool to her dusty feet. Her mind roved to one of the songs she had learned from Penny Dougherty.

All on one summer evening,
When the fevers were dawning,
I heard a fair maid make a mourn;
She was weeping for her father
And grieving for her mother
And thinking all on her true love John.

Without the square-paned windows, the musky earth lay under the hand of summer's sun. Garden rows were in view, rabbits and woodchucks fenced out by a wall of stones that mounted each year as more were turned from the ground. Blooming flowers were crowding outside the barrier, begonias, love-lies-bleeding, marigolds and sunflowers and honesty. Later sweet peas and corn poppies would flower, and nasturtiums and youth-and-old-age. Beyond were nestled the beehives, pale apple-blossom and maple honey already stored in the bottom super. In fall the hives would tower high and the men would rob them, carrying a pan of smoke. The topmost honey would be red-black, taken by the bees from buckwheat blooms. Anton would relish the high flavor, but Ellen would find it turning her stomach, like milk when the cows had eaten wild garlic.

In the early spring I dug in the clayey soil beside our small house and planted the seeds I knew. The land was different from the sandy earth I'd known beside the Great Lake. Here it clung to the hoe, sticky. I sang:

THEN YOU'LL REMEMBER ME

When o - ther lips and o - ther hearts Their tales of love shall tell in lan - guage whose ex-

cess im - parts the pow'r they feel so well, There may per - haps in such a scene some re - co - lec - tion be, of

days that have as ha - ppy been, And you'll re - me - m - ber me and you'll re - mem-ber, you'll re - me - m-ber me!

2
When coldness or deceit shall slight
The beauty now they prize,
And deem it but a faded light
Which gleams within your eyes,
When hollow hearts shall wear a mask,
'Twill break your own to see;
In such a moment I but ask
That you'll remember me,
That you'll remember, you'll remember me!

Our house and half-acre was set in a low place and when the rain began to pour it collected in a great pool and drowned all my young crop. It rained and rained, slowly filled our cellar, where my canned jams and pears and peaches and pickles were lined up on the shelves. Finally the jars were submerged and all the labels unglued and floated up. Later I had to guess and judge when I selected. Is this plum or grape jam? Strawberry or raspberry or gooseberry jelly?

A neighbor half-a-mile away lived in a house like mine. We liked each other easily. She was short and fat and had two small girls. She and her husband had whitewashed their tiny house when the winter had first gone. Now it stood gray-streaked, the boards drab again. She met me at the door. "It was worth it, if it only lasted a week," she said, "and our girls got to see it. Now it was a sight!"

Her two clung about her skirts like young chicks to a hen's wing. She gave me coffee in blue unmatching cups and saucers, and we talked. The rain came storming upon the windows of the small room. She told me she had once been tiny and pretty. "Then I married and I don't know what happened. Who knows?" She laughed without effort.

The thunder rumbled outside. "My garden's washed up," I sighed.

She told the children, "Hear that? It's the potato wagon going over the bridge."

"Sing us about Tennessee, Mamma."

WISH I WAS IN TENNESSEE

Wish I was in Tenn-e-ssee, Sit-ting in an ea-sy chair, My true love a-long my side, Comb-ing of her yel-low hair, Comb-ing of her yel-low hair!

2

Jaybird in an acorn tree,
Shaking acorns down,
My true love in a sugar tree
Shaking sugar down!

3

I went up on the hillside,
And give my horn a blow,
I thought I heard the birds a-calling
Yonder comes my beau!

"Why don't you give us one from up north," she said, "for them to hear. One with a story to it."

"We used to sing this one. It's got a happy ending, maybe."

THE RICH MAN AND ORPHAN GIRL

"No home, no home," cried an or-phan girl at the door to a rich man's hall, as she trem-bling stood on the mar-ble steps and leaned on the mar-ble wall.

2

The night was dark and the snow fell fast
As the rich man closed the door,
And his proud lips curled with scorn as he said,
"No bread, no room, for the poor!"

3

The rich man lay on his velvet couch
And he ate from plates of gold,
While the orphan girl on her bed of snow
Cried out, "So cold, so cold!"

4

The years went by and the rich man died,
He descended to fiery hell;
While the orphan girl lay in an angel's arms,
And sighed, "All's well, all's well!"

"Mercy," she said.

"I think it's better if you sing." I drank my chicory-tasting coffee, smiling.

"Well now, here's one I got from Grandma. These young ones can sing it too." And the girls joined her:

BIRD IN A GILDED CAGE

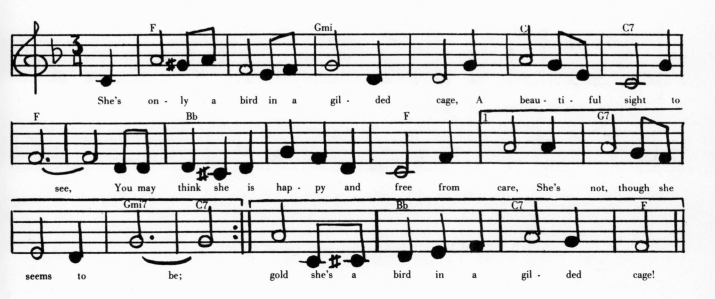

She's on-ly a bird in a gil-ded cage, A beau-ti-ful sight to
see, You may think she is hap-py and free from care, She's not, though she
seems to be; gold she's a bird in a gil-ded cage!

2

She sighs when she thinks of her wasted life,
For youth cannot mate with age,
Her beauty was sold for an old man's gold.
She's a bird in a gilded cage!

After a week the rain stopped. Everyone hired a pump from a man who went from house to house, clearing the water out. I gazed discouraged upon the hard-packed garden plot which was drying in the sun, caking and resistant.

My husband owned a truck and worked out for farmers sometimes for a share of the crop. He had heard of a widow who would rent her farm for a share and go to live in the town with her son. And so we contracted to her for a season. There was a pig house, and a place for chickens, a barn for milk cows. In the loft was a swing in the doorway, where one could sail out over the yard and look down the sweeping fertile fields, ours for the coming months.

The place had a rolling lawn and big-boled trees. The house was rambling, wind caught at the foundation stones and leaking windows in winter, finding a way through. My mother sent a pair of milking does and someone gave me a basket of tiny baby pigs to rear.

In the cellar was a monumental iron stove and a vast kettle to hold wash water, which was carried in from the pump. While it heated I put rice puddings and apples in honey and butter to bake in the oven. I was tired of wringing the sheets and diapers by hand, and in town shopped around and brought home a hand wringer, felt the luxury of the machine age. I pinned the clothes to the long rope, drawing the sheets tight, smoothing the pillow cases I'd once embroidered for a hope chest, on the advice of our Indiana cook in my childhood. My new baby boy slept in the sun.

I sang old-fashioned songs and felt my place in the wheel of time:

THE FOUR MARYS

Word is fro-m the kit-chen and word is from the hall, That Ma-ry Ham-il-ton drowned her babe by the high-est stew-ard of all!

2

Word is from the kitchen, and word is come to me,
That Mary Hamilton drowned her babe and throwed him into the sea.

3

Down did come the old queen, red tassels on her head,
"Mary Hamilton, where's the babe I saw lying in yonder bed?"

4

"Go put on your robes of black, go put on your robes of brown,
And you shall come and go with me to hang in old Edinborough
    Town."

5

"No, I won't put on my robes of black, nor yet my robes of brown,
And I'll put on my robes of white to hang in old Edinborough Town!

6

"Little did my mother think the day she cradled me,
Of the lands I was to travel in, and the death I was to see.

7
"Little did my father think when he sat me on his knee,
Of the seas I was to travel on, and the death that was to be.

8
"Last night there were four Marys; tonight there'll be but three,
There was Mary Beaton and Mary Seaton and Mary Carmichael and
     me!"

There was no electricity and we used candles in the house, and
kerosene lamps. The fuel stood in a can in the shed outside the door.
I was already familiar with its uses. In Michigan the hired man had
told me of its beneficial character, dousing his wounds with it when he
ripped his hand on a nail or cut his finger on the sickle. "Coal-oil can't
kill, and will likely cure," he declared. And he advised me to pour it
down any ailing animal's throat. As a small child I'd watched others
use the lamps that were sometimes the means of lighting the summer
houses we lived in. I'd seen the cotton wicks trimmed when the
flame grew uneven and sooted the shining chimneys. Candles I was
familiar with when storms hit the Michigan countryside and power
lines were down, for a few days at a time. It was pleasant to live with
their warmth and aliveness.

In the kitchen stood our three-burner oil stove as well as our
landlady's wood stove. The windows were large and in the daytime
the sun blazed through. Every now and then, stirred by the new way of
life there, I started a story, plotted it, and then called away by the busy
life, left it easily, not sufficiently involved.

My relatives came to visit, and brought cars or a truck-end of
bushels of beans and cucumbers and tomatoes. I put up what I had jars
for, and when they came to visit in a few days again, the daughter of
the old grandfather spotted a tall basket of tomatoes still standing.

"My! Throw them in the ditch quick," she said, "or set them
somewhere so Gramp can't see. He wants everything saved!"

The families of my relatives were close-knit and Catholic. I had
become a convert to the faith, eager, curious. My anxious Luxembourg
grandmother, Oma, had seen that I was baptized along with my sisters
at near seven years old. None of us had been given a middle name at
birth, and we all took hers, Mary Steichen, for ours.

These "cradle Catholics," born to their faith, were relaxed about
their religion, attending mass as a matter of course; they were used to
schedules in their daily living, milking and feeding. Wives would go
into town for the early six-o'clock so the husbands could care for the
children if need be and make a later mass. Or again husbands went
early, wives took the elder offspring and attended the sociable ten- or
eleven-o'clock masses. I followed their customs, wanting to submerge
myself in their mores.

My fat former neighbor came to visit our farm. She told me of
the tent preachers that set up outside the small towns, somewhere on
the road. She and the two girls walked the few miles down the highway

now and then to hear them on warm summer evenings or on Sunday
afternoons. They sang for me revival songs, evangelistic:

LIFE IS LIKE A MOUNTAIN RAILROAD

Life is like a moun-tain rail-road, with an en-gin-eer that's brave; We must make the run suc-

cess-ful From the cra-dle to the grave; Watch the curves. the fills, the tres-tles, Do not fal-ter, do not

fail; Keep your hand up-on the throt-tle, And your eye up-on the rail!

They clapped their hands in time to the rhythm, the way they
did in the tent shows while the saved walked up the aisle. They told
about one time when the preacher said, "Stand up for Jesus," and some
folks stayed sitting. He told them, "You can stand up for Jesus or get
the hell out of this meeting!"

TRAVELING ON

My hea-ven-ly home is bright and fair; I feel like trav-el-ing on; Nor pain nor death can

en-ter there; I feel like trav-el-ing on! Yes, I feel like trav-el-ing on, I

feel like trav-el-ing on; My hea-ven-ly home is bright and fair; I feel like trav-el-ing on!

I never heard religious songs from my Catholic relatives and friends. They were gentle and humorous about their beliefs and didn't force them upon me or each other. I had learned of this tolerance from my mother, who had left this church of her ancestors as a freethinking girl of sixteen. I put her experience in my first book and the reply of the Jesuit priest to whom she spoke:

> Then Ellen told the priest what was in her. And she added, "In the gospel of Matthew, the Lord himself says, don't pray where you're seen of men. But enter into thy closet. And when you've shut thy door, pray to thy Father which is in secret. And use not vain repetitions."
>
> The priest saw she loved God. He saw her mind was bright and she had thought this thing out. The wise Jesuit was not uncommon among those consecrated to the cross of his faith. He spoke to Ellen. "It's not your kind that need the mother church. We'll wait till you're ready to come again to us." And he told the girl's father, "Don't worry about your daughter, sir. She's in no danger of damnation. God is with her."

Sometimes dark tales were bruited of overburdened mothers confessing sins to priests who turned them out of the church, relentless, fearful of the modern trend. But I saw mainly large contented families, motherly children of nine and ten years who cared for their siblings casually.

Among the young people there was singing. I heard country tunes that told of betrayal and wounding, of villains. They sang of some old sea, of serpents, of a sweetheart who was shot for a swan; there were designing sisters, and cruel brothers, elder ones; there were queens, and then there was death, chief opponent in the strife. A few songs had happy endings; now and then a long-separated pair were reunited, more often not. But again and again and again, eternal love was vowed, its pain declared:

THE TRUE LOVERS' FAREWELL

As I walked out one cold win-ter's morn, A-drink-ing of sweet wine, A-lov-ing of that pret-ty young man that stole that heart of mine!

2
The crow is black, my love you know,
But it will turn to white;
If ever I do forsake you,
Bright day will turn to night!

3

Now don't you see that lonesome dove
That flies in so high degree?
And ain't it hard for me to die
For a man that don't love me?

4

I wish your breast was made of glass,
All in it I might behold,
Your name in secret I would write
In letters of fine gold.

5

I wish I was ten thousand miles,
Or on some distant shore,
Or down in some low valley place
Where the wild beasts howl and roar!

6

Did you see green grass tramped underfoot
Arise and grow again?
Love it is a killing thing,
Did you ever feel the pain?

Amid the tragedy and the heavy hearts were the gay young folks, the serene mothers, the strong fathers, the philosophizing grandmothers. There was the comfort of warm kitchen stoves and of food. For breakfast they set out great plates of fried potatoes and bacon and eggs, hot biscuits and large cups of coffee. I put a scene in my second book as I had witnessed it:

On the wedding day the peach trees in Job's orchard were just passing their full blow. The petals were shedding like pink snow on the emerald grass. The pee-wee birds complained all into the morning, and the spiders had spun early in the bushes. The meadowlarks flew high predicting fair weather. Everyone came in his finery, church and party clothes. In the yard where the turf was trampled by scuffling boots, food was being set on planks stretched over sawhorses and covered with Dolly's best tablecloths. Granny, Dolly's mother who lived with the Summers, had made sponge cakes out of baskets of eggs. She had frosted them with spun sugar and was cutting them with a silk thread, clucking. Square chocolate cakes stood out. Fudge half an inch thick had been poured over them, congealing in solid swirls. A great urn of boiled tea was there, and a bucket of hot coffee, the sack of ground beans floating in it. And there were pies; apple, peach, berry, with browned latticed tops, open custard ones that Faith's sisters had decorated with red jelly and fruit and curdled cream. Gooseberry tarts smelling like forget-menots. Puddings and compotes, apples stewed in whisky, crocks of potato salad, some hot and odored of fried bacon. A neighbor woman was slicing a huge roast with a blade that slid into the crackling skin and fat and rare

meat, and the red juice ran and puddled into the dish below. A thin tall
girl was sawing bread, spreading the slices with soft butter and chili sauce
or horseradish.

The young people clapped hands and sang:

I'LL GIVE TO YOU

I'll give to you an ea - sy chair to sit in while you comb your
gol - dy hair, If you will mar - ry me me me, If you will mar - ry me!

2
I'll give to you a dress of green
To make you look like Anne The Queen,
If you will marry me me me,
If you will marry me.

3
I'll give to you a silver spoon
To feed your baby in the afternoon . . .

4
I'll give to you a little lap dog
To carry with you when you go abroad . . .

5
I'll give to you a house and land,
Fifty head of cattle and a hired man . . .

6
Give to me the key to your chest
And all the money that you possess,
And I will marry you you you,
Yes, I will marry you!

7
Well, I can see that money is all
And the love of a man is nothing at all,
So I won't marry you you you,
I will not marry you!

Then I sang a song for them; they didn't care much for it. The
theme was too close; they weren't interested. I'd known the tune all
my life. Our father'd heard it as a young man in a small town to the

north of "Little Egypt," when he'd worked beside a milkman, washing eight- and ten-gallon delivery cans and quart measuring cups. I had used to roar it out in our dairy house in Michigan. I'd been a farmer by choice and I'd washed our milk cans by choice:

THE FARMER COMES TO TOWN

When the far-mer comes to town with his wa-gon bro-ken down, Oh, the far-mer is the man who feeds them all; If you'll on-ly look and see, I think you will a-gree, that the far-mer is the man who feeds them all. The far-mer is the man, the far-mer is the man, Buys on cre-dit till the fall; Then they take him by the hand and they lead him from the land, And the mer-chant is the man who gets it all!

2
The doctor hangs around, while the blacksmith heats his iron,
Oh, the farmer is the man who feeds them all;
The preacher and the cook go strolling by the brook,
And the farmer is the man who feeds them all.

Out on the land the green turned to gold and the fields waved their banners of grain. The farmers rented a great combine which went from one to another, contracted far ahead of time. I stared at the monster, there in the sweet-odored ripe gold. My husband and brother-in-law sighed and allowed me to run the machine once, star-eyed, around the field. The sun blazed hot. The wheat was cut and the sheaves bound and the grain poured like honey behind me. I sang at the top of my voice, which was covered by the racket of the metal beast:

PHARAOH'S ARMY

Who's that com - ing, all dressed in red? One of the peo - ple that Pha - raoh led. For Pha - raoh's ar - my got drown - ded, Oh Ma - ry, don't you weep. Oh Ma - ry don't you weep, don't you morn, Pha - raoh' - ll come and take you home, For Pha - raoh's ar - my got drown - ded, Oh Ma - ry, don't you weep!

2
Tallest tree in Paradise,
The Christians call it the tree of life! . . .

3
If I'd have died when I was young,
I wouldn't of had this race to run . . .

4
Some of these days about four o'clock,
This old world is gonna reel and rock . . .

5
Some of these days, but I don't know when,
This old world is gonna end . . .

6
Go away, Satan, and let me be,
You fooled my brother but you can't fool me . . .

7
Satan wears a sinful shoe,
If you don't mind, he'll slip it on you . . .

8
Hain't been to heaven, but I been told,
The streets are pearly and the gates are gold . . .

9
When I get to heaven, gonna sit right down,
Wear a white robe and a starry crown . . .

The men motioned to me to go around again, and I guided the way of the machine, the sun a gold flower in the blue sky and smelling sweet as the grain. I shouted out a song of Woody Guthrie's, remembering the words of the poet in my childhood home who said:

The people is Everyman, everybody.
Everybody is you and me and all others.
What everybody says is what we all say.
And what is it we all say? . . .
Why should Everyman be lost for words?

THIS LAND IS YOUR LAND

This land is your land, this land is my land, from the Cal - i for - nia to the New York Is - land, from the red - wood for - est to the gulf - stream wa - ters, This land was made for you and me!

2
As I went walking that ribbon of highway,
I saw above me that endless skyway,
I saw below me that golden valley,
This land was made for you and me.

3
I roamed and rambled, and I followed my footsteps,
To the sparkling sands of her diamond deserts,
All around me a voice was sounding,
This land was made for you and me.

4
When the sun come shining, then I was strolling,
And the wheat fields waving, and the dust clouds rolling,
A voice was chanting as the fog was lifting,
This land was made for you and me!

PART FOUR

. . . By the rivers of Babylon . . . we hanged
our harps upon the willows in the midst
thereof. For there they that carried
us away captive required of us a song . . .
saying, Sing us one of the songs of Zion . . .

—PSALM 137

Things had happened out upon the land. A war came and passed; everyone was touched; no one escaped. I went back, with my children, to my parents' house. The Marines assaulted Guadalcanal in the hot summer of 1942; two years later the Allies invaded France, a thousand planes and gliders dropping men upon the old country. Less than a year later came Iwo Jima, and in short time, V-E Day, and in August the atom bomb shattering Hiroshima. F.D.R. had died and the Vice President was the new chief. He said that war was over on the last day of August in 1945.

My family had moved by then to a new state in the South. In the way of women, I had turned my eyes from the battling of men, and bent myself shuddering upon the earth. I tended it; I dug samples to see if it needed superphosphate, potash, borax. Should the alfalfa seed go in in fall or spring; should the ground be worked up first? Should we get this kind of tractor or that? We were in the west hill country of North Carolina and there were over two hundred acres of the land; much was mountain and woods, and of arable fields and pastures there were forty acres.

On the day we arrived, I had gone to the barns and met the old overseer coming up from the meadow with his oxen. He sat on top of the grassy hay stacked on the cart, and resembled a patriarch divorced from any world I had known. He was my first introduction to the mountain people; nothing hurried him. Serene, he let the pace of the handsome pair of brown oxen be his own. The beasts had a power in snaking trees from the woods surpassing any mule or horse, and for maneuverability, tractors. They were secure on treacherous mountain paths. They lived well and stayed sleek on meadow grass which had no nourishing clover and lezpedeza mixed in it.

Connemara was the name of our new home, set on its high hill by Christopher Gustavus Memminger, Secretary of the Confederate Treasury, about a hundred years before we made it ours. There were grandfather trees, well cared for, hollies, pines and oaks, mountainous outgrown boxwoods trimmed in formal fashion. There were water lilies flourishing on the lake down in front of the house, and beside its little bridge was a weatherbeaten sign: NURSES AND CHILDREN NOT ALLOWED AROUND LAKE. The water came from a big open spring on top of the mountain; it followed the old-fashioned line of pipes buried beside the trail on the way down. Sometimes the pipes would freeze and burst when there was a record cold winter, we were told. I wanted a two-way light switch in the basement through the vault-like room of book stacks to the tool-bench that I loved. At my request, our hardware man diagrammed the system, and blowing a fuse now and then, screwdriver and pliers in my jeans back pocket, I was amazed to find it could so easily be hitched up.

Patriots at once, we learned an ancient Southern warlike song, and quoted to each other from the Epilogue to Tennyson's "Charge of the Heavy Brigade":

The song that nerves a nation's heart
Is in itself a deed:

THE BONNIE BLUE FLAG

We are a band of bro-thers and na-tive to the soil, Fight-ing for our li-ber-ty with trea-sure, blood and toil; And when our rights were threa-tened the cry rose near and far: "Hur-rah for the Bon-nie Blue Flag that bears a sin-gle star! Hur-rah! Hur-rah! for South-ern rights, hur-rah! Hur-rah for the Bon-nie Blue Flag that bears a sin-gle star!

2
As long as the old Union was faithful to her trust,
Like friends and like brothers, kind were we and just,
But now that Northern treachery attempts our rights to mar,
We'll hoist on high the Bonnie Blue Flag that bears a single star!
Hurrah! Hurrah! for Southern rights, hurrah!
Hurrah for the Bonnie Blue Flag that bears a single star!

We kept the name Connemara, and registered it for the prefix of the goat herd. The animals wandered out onto the unfamiliar fields, cropping fresh grass that before they'd only tasted as dried hay. They moved in a group, following a leader, goat or human, easily. We set up new gates and fences and a tiny cinderblock dairy house. There to the clatter of pails in the steam, I sang the new songs we were learning, born in this land.

Here the people were still carrying on their only war, the old one; it stayed close to them. They let alone the First and Second World Wars and those before and in between; they preferred to nurse the hurt done in their time of trouble when the country was young and a row had started among themselves to settle whether states would act separately or as one.

Older families could remember how their relatives were rooted out of Charleston homes as that city was laid low. They fled to their Flat Rock summer homes here, and some eked out a livelihood on crops they grew. The Yankees came through these mountains, pillaging, and local bushwhackers engaged in guerrilla techniques. The mountaineers had divided their loyalties; some told of houses that sheltered in their lofts a boy in gray one week and one in blue the next.

There was a song made then in a deep anger by a people unable to accept a brother conqueror:

I WON'T BE RECONSTRUCTED

I'm a good old re-bel, and that's just what I am, And for this land of free-dom I do not care a damn; I'm glad we fought a-gainst her, I on-ly wish we'd won, And I don't ask no par-don for a-ny-thing I've done!

2

I served with old Bob Lee for three years near about,
Got wounded in four places, and starved at Point Lookout;
I caught the rheumatism from camping in the snow,
But I killed a sight of Yankees, and I wished I'd killed some more.

3

I hate the Constitution, the great Republic too,
I hate the mighty Eagle and the uniform of blue,
I hate the glorious banner and all the flags and fuss,
Those lying thieving Yankees, I hate them worse and worse.

We had brought dogs with us, and cats, and soon got more. I went down into Florida to judge a goat show and came back with a great Doberman Pinscher called Leif, and a Siamese cat, Sa-Wang. We had other dogs soon: cockers, Jackson and Hannah; my sister's collie, Shawn; and a lumbering Great Dane, Christopher.

There were little animals too, some for the kitchen, some pets. A small greenhouse was attached to the living room, and beneath it we built pens. Here a flock of rabbits lived, and after a while we added guinea pigs, short-haired ones, and a roseate variety with swirled hair, and later a shaggy white Abyssinian male called Teddy, shipped from a cavy-breeder in California. The house cats were registered Siamese, and I used the old Michigan name, Chikaming, for the prefix, began breeding bluepoints and sealpoints and establishing the Chikaming Cattery.

In the spirit of wanderers to new lands, nomadic, we still kept the various songs of independence we had latched onto in the gay days when we emptied the house in Michigan and loaded boxcars and vans that set forth for the mountains down here. As I trudged over to the barn, I was singing over and over our stanza from *The Beggar's Opera:*

ROAMING FREE AS THE BREEZE

Roam - ing free as the breeze, Who's to stop me and why? I live as I please, O - pen road, o - pen sky!

There stood our mother, trying to understand what the herdsman's little daughter was complaining about. But I heard clearly, as though she spoke a foreign tongue, what the child said. "Tha-o-ooster-ow-chandry-flawg-mi!" Or, "That old rooster out yonder flogged me!"

I translated, "The rooster attacked her, flapping its wings!"

"Is that what she says happened?"

The people used our language differently. I crossed the barnyard to where the carpenters were putting in partitions for the goats, and one of the men called out, "Hey!" In my land of Michigan that was a call of warning or salute; I was startled. Here it was their friendly greeting like the Michigander's cool, "Hi."

And I would hear the herdsman telling the goat Primavera, who was stubborn and would not turn about, "Swap ends, goat."

Back at the house the cook sighed, "Tell, where does the food-chopper live?"

I said, "In among that mess of pans in that drawer."

She protested, "No, I doubt it would be comfortable in there."

"Well."

She was mountain-bred, part Indian, and brought young poke-weed greens for herself, using grease to prepare them. She scrambled fresh eggs and mixed the greens in them. "Sure is good," she smiled.

I was becoming giddy with the spring and its passion. The rains were finished, and in the hills was sweet-smelling soggy spring. We sent off impossible seed orders, dug in the dirt, walked under the stars, became heady with the secret scent of hyacinths and daffodils. I kept a journal, spotting birds: cardinals and bluebirds, nuthatches, song sparrows, wrens, creepers, robins and jays, a few buzzards and crows. By the end of March the Tiger Swallowtail butterflies and the Hairstreaks were seen for almost two weeks. The daffodils and narcissi faded; the purple magnolia was in its high bloom. Shadblows, like drifts of cotton, appeared all over the big mountain behind us where a few tiny leaves unrolled themselves, green, yellow, red-tinted. By the beginning of May, phoebes, goldfinches, whippoorwills were sighted and heard whistling.

"Before sunrise on the first of May," declared the herdsman, "you got to have in all squash, cucumbers, watermelon, gherkins, pumpkins, melons, and such-like."

"I know. You're telling me! I know about the Man of Signs."

"Sure to God," he said pleased, and went for his hoe.

I had read my almanac, and saw eye to eye with him. There were twelve signs of the zodiac and each related to a part of the body. The signs ruled planting, breeding, butchering; farmers often heeded them; it did no harm to play with luck.

By the middle of the month the first mockingbird ever heard by the family was singing. We had known its coarse-voiced cousin, the catbird, in Michigan, as friendly, as curious, as persistent for attention. The new voice was satisfying. We got all sorts of chickens: Barred Rocks and Buff Orpingtons, the roosters huge. We got fancy breeds: the Rose-comb Black Minorca. We got Leghorns too, now and then, slim and bred for egg production not meat. We had ducks: white Pekings and a few half-tame Muscovies, wheeling over fences and flying up to Janet's hand and call. There were geese, and after a while bees. The constant tide of laden golden-brown Italian bees went in and out of the white oblong hives.

Delighted with the bee project, I went about in my secondhand bee regalia: white coveralls and head net, long canvas gloves. I was never stung. And in the fashion of farms our honey came all at once; we cut it into squares, the honey running out of the wax; we stuffed it into jars, set it out in plates on the table. Nothing arrived in an orderly way; all was profusion.

There would be mammoth crops of roses and strawberries set out in bowls. And as the roses began to let up, the pink huge rhododendrons were bursting down by the front gate, in the woods, on the hills everywhere. They were spectacular and as strange as the mockingbird to just-arrived foreigners.

"I never saw flowers like that in my life!" I gasped to the cook.

"Yankee," she said good-humoredly, "what's it like up in the north country?"

I wanted to make the mountain behind our home my own. I set out to find the name of each flower that bloomed, each insect that moved, each bird that sang. In the same way I had known the sand-dune country of Michigan and had collected Lepidoptera, pressed wild flowers, leaves, evergreen needles, and looked them up in books, writing down the Latin and common names, and hung them in cases. I wanted to name each star that shone, each planet that circled and gleamed. I called the names: Woodsorrels, Blackeyed Susans, Touchmenots that were yellow and spurred and tall. Black Walnuts, Cottonwoods, Trembling Aspens, White Pines and Hemlocks, the needles lustrous green above, and pale below. Castor, Pollux, Antares, the beautiful Vega, and the brightest one of all: the Dog Star. And Venus and Jupiter and red-orange Mars, green-splotched and mysterious.

And I sang songs, walking about the mountain, scrambling up, catching roots for finger and toe hold, and sliding down, splashing through springs and creek-beds, and sunning on moss-grown rock expanses, sometimes a quarter-mile long. One song was a Welsh tune we'd been taught:

I COULD NOT FIND MY BABY, OH!

2

I followed the trail of the yellow fawn, yellow fawn, yellow fawn,
I followed the trail of the yellow fawn,
But I could not find my baby, oh!

3

I followed the wee brown otter's track, otter's track, otter's track,
I followed the wee brown otter's track,
But I could not find my baby, Oh!

4

I followed the trail of the mountain mist, mountain mist, mountain mist,
I followed the trail of the mountain mist,
But I could not find my baby, Oh!

In the same way that there was overabundance of roses and rhododendrons and strawberries and honey, there was a season of over-supplies of milk. And so we made cheeses and stored them.

Some were begun in the heated steamy little greenhouse. There the green-yellow lettuce spears grew, the tomatoes, the tiny winter garden. There the bread dough was set to rise, and there in a pail my special cheese ripened. It was turned with a wood spoon every day for a week or so until it changed its character, from a white dry farmer's curd to a smooth yellow mass.

The cook turned away. "Will your cheeses taste like they smell!"

At the same time that the lettuce was watered, the cheese was stirred. Then the pail was taken to the kitchen one day and the stuff dumped in a buttered iron pan and cooked a little. Now it was bland and anise or other herb could be added, or nuts, or cream. It was poured into jars, to be relished with the baked bread, the new-churned butter, a bowl of berries, a glass of goat milk, hot coffee; that was our supper.

Busy, I paused at the front door to glance out onto the porch where stood the make-believe Mr. McGillicuddy, who looked off to the distant high blue hills, and who always wore the same hat. It had come from an old family friend, a Lincoln collector, who had been restrained from throwing it out and had given it to our father. Sometimes the hat sat on a chairback on top of a sweater, with a pair of empty hiking shoes sprawled under the chair. Sometimes it sat on top of a three-pronged tall stick brought in from the woods. But the hat marked the mythical creature as Michael McGillicuddy and we snapped his photograph, fond.

My two children came up behind me, hand in hand, their tiny trenchcoats and rainhats matching. It was the peaceful pre-school time, before the girl and boy understood that the sexes warred. Not until they were in their late teens would they be again at such concord with each other. The girl-child, Paula, cautioned me regarding her doll, Sally Ann:

"Hush. Her's asleep in she's cradle."

And the boy warned, "Don't touch a thing on the table in our room. I'm making a picture."

"What is it?"

"I'm drawing God."

"No one knows what he looks like, silly."

"They'll know when I get through, Helga."

The pair went by me, onto the porch. They nodded to Mr. Mc-Gillicuddy as they passed him, going down the steps and wandering on the path, heading for the woodshed or the old dairy house or the pig pen up on the mountainside. They sang tunes sometimes without understanding the words, accepting them. I recognized my own errors.

My nice have seen the golore of the coming of the Lord!

He has trampled out the vintage where the drapes are rather stored.

They sang of the cross-eyed bear:

Gladly the cross I'll bear!

And of the three on that old night:

Silent night, holy night,

All is calm, all is bright;

Round John Virgin, mother, and child!

They spent time with their grandfather, whom they dubbed Buppong. He in turn gave them names; the yellow-haired girl became Snick, and the red-haired boy, christened another name, became John. The three made up songs while I was busy doing what I wanted to do, cleaning out barns, shearing winter coats from the goats, buying a new mare to explore the mountain above us. When I came back they shouted at me:

BALLAD

Do you re-mem-ber sweet Snick from Con - ne - mara Who crossed the con-fluence with her bro-ther John? With Leif and with Han-nah and two gui-nea pigs, They made the trip in an old yel-low rig.

2
When they got down as far as the store
They were so tired they couldn't go any more,
So they turned around and towards home they did go,
With the dogs and the pigs and the rig going slow!

Coming home with me later from the nursery school in the close-by village, the big dog Christopher in the seat between them, they hung words on the tune, "Tipperary."

IT'S A SHORT WAY

G
It's a short way to Connemara,
    C   G
It's a short way to go,
It's a short way to Connemara,
         D7
And the nicest goats I know!

G
Goodbye, County Court House,
C D7
Farewell, Hatch's Feed Store;
G C G
It's a short way to Connemara,
D7 G
And we're just about there!

The boy-child was four, and I complained one morning as I jerked his sweater upon him. "I never saw the like. Can't you dress yourself yet!"

He was calm. "You shouldn't shove a yitta child around like that."

"You're a baby!" I ridiculed.

He retaliated with easy scorn, "Did you ever see a baby run an electric train, Helga?"

His sister was three, and as they turned away from me, they started to chant what they'd learned from the herdsman's daughters in the nearby house:

OLD DAM TUCKER

G
Old Dam Tuck - er was a fine old man, Washed his face in a
D7 G D7 G
fry - ing pan, Combed his hair with a wa - gon wheel, And he died with a tooth-ache in his heel!

2
Go get out of the way for Old Dam Tucker,
He's too late to get his supper,
Get out of the way for Old Dam Tucker
He's too late to get his supper.

3
Old Dam Tucker was down in town,
Riding a goat and leading a hound,
The hound gave a howl, the goat gave a jump,
And Old Dam Tucker fell straddle on a stump!

They kept mixing up the words. I didn't straighten them out quickly. There was plenty of time for that; a lifetime.

I gave my love to a cherry what had no stone,
I gave my love to a baby what had no crying!

They went around quoting A. A. Milne, who mixed things up: " 'Well,' said Owl, 'the customary procedure in such cases is as follows.' 'What does Crustimoney Proseedcake mean?' said Pooh, 'for I am a Bear of Very Little Brain, and Long Words bother me.' "

They sang:

SKIP TO MY LOU

2
Buppong's hat got torn in two!

3
Snick's pretty as a redbird and a bluebird too!

4
All around the house, skip to my Lou!

Buppong, as master of the household, took their education seriously. He told them, "There's no law against a man believing in the unbelievable."

Their grandmother was away speaking at a goat meeting; Margaret was practicing the piano; Janet was feeding kids at the barn; I sat in the farm office at my typewriter, half-listening to the three while I answered letters from prospective customers who wanted to buy kids from our best milkers, and while I typed goat pedigrees to enclose with the replies. He explained first that he'd flunked out of West Point because of poor Math grades; then he coached the two who were not yet of an age to go to grammar school in Arithmetic. He set them problems to study out:

"First problem. There were two one-legged men in a room. One of them had cropped ears. How many men were in the room?"

"That's hard, Buppong," they squealed.

"Second problem. There was a zebra with five stripes on one side and six on the other. He got sick and lost a stripe. How many were left?"

He was reading mail; they slit it open for him: letters, magazines, papers, advertisements. He told them, "Some men when they get mad get drunk. I read the newspapers."

"He's fooling," John told Snick.

"You can't tell," she said.

"He's powerful."

"Sure," and she said, "Stand up, Buppong." He obeyed. "Sit down. Stand up. Sit down. Stand up. Sit down. Now you can stay."

"That's a powerful mountain out there," John told Buppong. "To carry all those toadstools and trees on its back."

"True, Johnny-me-old-friend-John."

And they began to carefully fill in letters that arrived from advertising concerns wanting information. *Nature of firm's business.* Kids and Milk. *Your title*: Poobah. *Signature*: Heathcliffe Flummadummer.

The herdsman came through the room and into my office to speak with me about a fellow who had a little spring wagon to sell, just right for the new pony. The herdsman glanced at where the three sat about the table. "That little girl is purely in the aping stage," he told me.

"You're right."

Snick was arranging her grandfather's pencils in a can, and repeating his enunciation with false solemnity. "The road . . . to hell . . . is paved . . . with good intentions . . . war is war . . . peace is peace . . . if all nations . . . would settle their differences . . . each must sacrifice . . . some principle . . . the fog comes . . . on little kitty feet . . . it sits looking . . . over city and harbor . . . on silent haunches . . . and then moves on . . . that's all . . . that's all . . !"

As we went past and out to the barn, their voices followed, the strong deep one and the two small ones:

I DREAMT THAT I DWELT IN MARBLE HALLS

In the barnyard I didn't say much. The fellow was asking twenty dollars. "That's a lot," I commented, placid.

And the herdsman suggested, "Tell you what. We'll give you ten, and all the rock you can pick out of that rye field."

"It's a deal," the fellow said.

As we took a look at our new spring wagon, I asked the herdsman, "What's he want with rock?"

"I knew he needed it for the underpinning of a house he's putting up."

I liked trading. I liked horse-dealing. We had a steady procession of them. There was the black-and-white pony, Patches, whom we brought home in the station wagon. There were Storm and Blueberry and Paper Doll and Bess and her black foal, and Gray Boy and Remember and a wonderful wild one called Daniel. When we wanted to trade Daniel, the herdsman and I worked in collusion, disguising his flighty ways, his undependability, emphasizing his style and handsome racking gait. We made a pretty good bargain, all told.

I loved the style of horses; there was not an ungraceful one. The gray work team Pearl and Major, like living statues, moved up and down the black plowed fields, and snaked logs from the woods for winter firewood, dragged the roads to make them smooth. We put red roses or zinnias in the bridles of the riding horses, at their temples, as we went back and forth, on errands, and for a lark.

I rode the saddle horse Storm, down to the post office for the afternoon mail and brought it to the house. Snick welcomed me, shrill, from the window, "Good Helga! Nice person."

And I called back, "Nice daughter," dismounting and coming in.

Buppong was reading to John, who stood mounted on stilts of tall tomato juice cans, a rope looped in each hand, the ends fastened to the cans, holding them to his feet. He wore a disheveled old hat of his grandfather's with a rooster feather threaded through a couple of holes in it. Snick, on the window sill, swung her feet.

Paper is two kinds, to write on, to wrap with.
If you like to write, you write.
If you like to wrap, you wrap.
Some papers like writers, some like wrappers.
Are you a writer or a wrapper?

"He's silly," said Snick, delighted.

Buppong looked over at me. "We three ain't got no dignity." He grinned, and ordered the girl-child, "Pour your mother a scups-coffee." She ran swiftly to the kitchen.

I sat with them a little while, helped to open the late mail, and reported on the spring wagon for Patches. Then I stood, sipping the last of the coffee. "There's an hour before milking time, and I have some things to do." I was heading, shy, for my room and my secret journals and poems. "I'll see you at supper, Buppong."

He sliced his cigar in two and put the stub in his teeth and shrugged. "Write till you're ashamed of yourself, girl."

"I know."

He had turned back to the children, and was drawling up to the child on the can-stilts beside his chair, "Allow me, as Lincoln used to say, the Yankee privilege of answering your question by first asking one myself."

"Why not?" said the boy, saucy.

"Let's bind him hand and foot," said the girl, "and watch him struggle."

"Go fetch the rope," ordered their grandfather, "I'm not unwilling."

I had closed the doors between us and was at my desk, the black binder open. About on the walls were brash paintings. Lately I had started them, coaxing a sister or child to sit, sometimes catching Buppong at his mail. Sometimes I painted the herdsman's handsome child. I framed a cartoon and put it on the wall under them; a painter is defending his art to a small boy. "It just so happens I don't care what you think!"

My uncle, Steichen, looked at my things and said, "Unless you're willing to turn your life over to it, you won't be any good." And he handed me a book on Modigliani and unwrapped a Ben Shahn to hang on my wall.

He had come visiting Connemara, and the farm was paraded before his properly surprised eyes. Snick, by now turning five, came galloping past him on her horse Remember, and he whispered, "She's like a butterfly perched on that beast!"

In the evening we sat in the living room, some of us on the floor. John blew on the harmonica and the men nodded over his head, "The young fellow has talent."

Grandfather, granduncle and the children had spent the afternoon busily picking over and selecting buckeyes from under the tree down the drive. They were a shining polished brown, inedible, ornamental; they were heaped in a candy dish on the fireplace mantel.

Steichen went about with the buckeyes. "Have a chocolate. Do!"

He pretended to eat one himself, appreciating the flavor, getting a small bit of chocolate stuck in a back tooth. He tried unsuccessfully for a while to extract it, and finally to his and everyone's relief, did so, smiling sweetly. No one else ate a bonbon; Buppong put his away for later; Grandma refused; Margaret claimed she was on a diet; and Janet shook her head:

"I have to feed kids. Does anyone want to come see?"

"Me for one," said our uncle.

And we trooped on Janet's heels, down to watch. She let out six of the tiny week-old beasts at a time. They scampered bleating to the feeding rack, where she had measured into the tin dishes their milk, heated to the right degree. They sucked it all with noisy slurps, butting the pans, hoping for more. Then Janet washed each one's face and they went dashing before her in a troop, the long ears of the Nubians flopping, back to their straw-bedded stable room, next to the furnace.

117

We returned upstairs to the sitting room. It was dusk and we got the guitar from the corner. Then Steichen taught us a homemade song he'd conjured up, patriotic, about his particular state:

CONNECTICUT EATS THE NUTMEG

We had to admit we had no such wonderful original tune, and so we loudly rendered an old-timer about our new land for which our patriotism grew stronger each year:

THE GOOD OLD NORTH STATE

Before I wound my way to bed, on the heels of my sleepy children, I sang with the rest the anti-war song I'd heard back in my earliest childhood:

I DON'T WANT TO BE BURIED IN THE STORM

I don't want to be bur-ied in the storm, Oh Lord -y! I don't want to be bur-ied in the storm, Oh an - gel, oh an - gel, I don't want to be bur-ied in the storm!

2
Dig my grave with a golden spade,
Oh Lordy!
Dig my grave with a golden spade,
Oh angel, oh angel,
Dig my grave with a golden spade!

3
Winding sheet going to hold me fast!

4
Lower me down with a silken chain!

Some time in the night I woke to hear the two men still talking. They were out on the front porch. There on the boards the moonlight from the mountains met the yellow lamplight from the farm office where our mother worked. Buppong was doing favorite exercises, vigorously hoisting chairs up over his head and setting them back down. Then he was stretching and twisting, while Steichen sat back and watched.

"I don't mind going for a walk," my uncle said, "but bending my index finger's enough exercise for me."

The flow of their voices lulled me. I could occasionally hear our mother's movements as she got up from her chair in the farm office, to pull open a file drawer or to clatter on the typewriter. Vigorous, enthusiastic, she moved through the days of my life. She let me grow up freely, my decisions my own, so that my life around her was bright. Wise, I followed her ways, and like a mother bear, turned my own children loose early.

She planted great kitchen gardens on the new farm, resurrected old rose groupings, trimmed the boxwoods, planted flowers about the house and along the fence that looked to the mountains. I saw her stand sometimes, quiet and withdrawn, looking at some beast or plant. And soon she would speak, decisive.

"This buck needs more exercise. Let's put him in the Lower Pasture." Or she said, "It is too shady here for these Chinese forget-menots. Next spring we'll put them by the Rock Garden."

I knew my father had written in poems about her:

> *. . . I have hunted you under my thoughts,*
> *I have broken down under the wind*
> *And into the roses looking for you.*
> *I shall never find any greater than you.*

He had spoken of her in free verse, saying that people wrote poetry because they wanted to.

> *. . . Your hands are sweeter than nut-brown bread*
> *When you touch me. . . .*

I wanted to write a poem for her and did, scribbling it out and putting it back in a drawer for a while.

ELOGE TO MY MOTHER

> *This small-boned powerful life-loving woman*
> *Views the world and us her children introspectively.*
> *With disheveled chatter and disposition even*
> *To us she is certain sanctuary.*
>
> *When she goes with odorous straw to make*
> *A bed for those small goats she loves,*
> *They fall kneeling among her beautiful hands that take*
> *Strongly apart the oat bales interwove.*
>
> *They adore her! And when they set about*
> *To drop their young, they press against her side,*
> *Their calls of agony not so great a shout*
> *As if she were not there to hear they cried.*
>
> *I would send her all my love this way,*
> *In a ranting and incompleted poem,*
> *Attempting with industry not as a small child to say,*
> *"Love!" But as a woman not too well or wisely grown.*
>
> *Somehow in whatever house this gray-eyed one keeps*
> *In haphazard absentminded disarray,*
> *One ear is tuned to window where the locust Acridiidae leaps,*
> *And to her addresses a private roundelay.*
>
> *About on tables and sills crowd blooming hypnotized flowers.*
> *Her left hand tends them, her right holds a political treatise.*
> *Her notions are Greek-founded, yet laid in present hours,*
> *Concerned and absolute for her country's true increase.*

On a dim wall is framed a baby in fine yellowed lace
Upon an ample long-dressed sunlit lap.
A smile of pleasure wreathes the tiny face,
Surfeit of sleep and food and warmth in my crocheted cap.

When time moved and she came once to visit me,
We had to buy a dozen varied saplings for she said,
"You can't have a yard without a tree!"
From the cellar I got up a pick and a man's stout spade.

The rocks had been created one with the soil
And to make a root-basin properly
Took a half hour's steady toil.
"Here," she said, and grasped my tool, "Let me

Dig that hole. My body's old
And doesn't matter longer. You are young!"
Helpless, half-astonished I stood.
She heaved and chopped, the boulders flung.

The cave was built forthwith. I would send
Her all my love, knowing she has no patience or place
In her valiant person for tribute. Still I would commend
To her retiring self, enormous processionals of praise.

Certain days we marked on our calendar: *Goldfinch seen in the pink dogwood. Guinea pig Betsey bred by Porky.* When the rain stopped there was a robin storm: *Counted over 40 Redbreasts. Fog had kittens in hall closet. 33 Purple Finches on bird station.* And in the herdsman's scrawl when the black colt was born: *Bess folded.*

There were tragic notations too: *Christopher proved sheepkiller.* My Great Dane had been got as a mature beast from the vet and was tender and jolly with the children and other dogs. Then one day Christopher wasn't at the milking-room door where he always waited on me. When I called, there came a distant bark. I dashed to the hill overlooking the buck kid pasture, and saw the torn strewn bodies. Calling Christopher to heel, I asked the herdsman to take his collar and lock him away in the chicken house; I never wished to see him again; the vet would come for him. And I issued a beating to the Doberman, Leif, yet a pup, in terror lest he follow the older dog's lesson. None of the attacked bucklings were saved. One curled beside me, his head on my knees; he was conscious, his throat ragged only slightly, with little loss of blood. He was expensive, imported from a British Saanen herd, a favorite, handsome and white. The vet was patient with my protestations. "Please, Doc."

"It's the shock kills them. There's not a thing more I can do."

On the summer nights we rode in the moon-loved Carolina state, the metal horseshoes clashing upon the stones of the roads, sounding into the century-old trees hovering above, their shadows cast ahead. We were humming old songs, sung a thousand thousand times:

THE SHIP THAT NEVER RETURNED

On a sum-mer's day when the waves were rip-pling with a quiet and gen-tle breeze, A ship set sail with a

car - go la -den for a port be -yond the seas. Did she ev - er re - turn? No, she ne - ver re -turned, and her

fate is still un -learned, But a last poor man set sail com -man -der On the ship that ne -ver re - turned.

2

There were sad farewells, there were friends forsaken,
And her fate is still unlearned,
But a last poor man set sail commander
On the ship that never returned.

3

Said a feeble lad to his aged mother,
"I must cross that deep blue sea,
For I hear of a land in a far-off country,
Where there's health and strength for me."

4

" 'Tis a gleam of hope and a maze of danger,
And our fate is still to learn,"
And a last poor man set sail commander
On the ship that never returned.

5

Said a feeble lad to his aged mother,
As he kissed his weeping wife,
"Just one small purse of that golden treasure,
It will last us all through life."

6

"Then we'll live in peace and joy together
And enjoy all I have earned."
So they sent him forth with a smile and a blessing
On the ship that never returned!

And one at a time the children became five and before long six and were going to grammar school in the village. They were coming home with unchanged rhymes I had once used and forgot, songs to choose sides with, to jump rope to, or to use for making decisions:

CINDERELLA

Cinderella dressed in yellow,
Went upstairs to see her fellow;
How many kisses did she get?
1, 2, 3, 4, 5 . . .

Cinderella dressed in lace,
Went upstairs to powder her face;
How many boxes did she use?
1, 2, 3, 4, 5 . . .

Cinderella dressed in green,
Went upstairs to eat ice cream;
How many dishes did she eat?
1, 2, 3, 4, 5 . . .

MONKEY, MONKEY

Monkey, monkey, bottle of beer,
How many monkeys are there here?
1, 2, 3, 4, 5, 6, 7,
All good children go to heaven!

1, 2, 3, 4, 5, 6, 7,
All good children go to heaven,
When they get there they will shout,
"O,U,T," and that spells out!

TEDDY BEAR, TEDDY BEAR

Teddy bear, teddy bear, turn around,
Teddy bear, teddy bear, touch the ground,
Teddy bear, teddy bear, go upstairs,
Teddy bear, teddy bear, say your prayers.

Which had its variations:

Butterfly, butterfly, throw a kiss,
Butterfly, butterfly, get out before you miss.

Buster, buster, hands on your head,
Buster, buster, go to bed!

Johnny, Johnny, what's the price of geese?
Johnny, Johnny, fifty cents a piece;
Johnny, Johnny, that's too dear,
Johnny, Johnny, get out of here!

A lot of my time was spent up in the blue hills, with one friend or another, talking to people we met casually, or knew. We rode the horses and let Bess's colt come alongside. It tired easily, and lay down at the summit in the sun. We had to wait until it would consent to shamble to its feet and follow the mare again.

One man we met told of how a Bible salesman had gone from door to door the past week, selling handsome editions, gold-embossed, gold-edged. In some sections the first letter was immense, with doves or flowers set into scrolled lines. They were such bargains that he and a number of his neighbors bought them gladly. Later they found that many sections were missing.

"I hunted for Jeremiah to no avail," he told us. "He's my favorite prophet. And the Book of John wasn't there. Or Kings or Isaiah!"

Back in the hills the families sat in their chairs before dirt-floored cabins, on the rough turf, or tilted them back on the sloped frow-hewn wood porches. Some were pale-faced, few with the hardy healthy faces of their ancestors, a look of inbreeding about them. The women tired and aged early; the men were not too huge, often stooped, leathery-faced. All from the littlest to the eldest had an inimitable kind of independence, which shone like a bright light from their brittle blue or black eyes. The ballads were mourned, often in a high minor tone, the voices thin and untrained and positive.

One day I waited in the sunshine on my mare, for the colt, half-asleep, who refused to be roused by the anxious Doberman beside him. He flicked his ears, gazed mildly at the whining Leif, and sighing stretched out on his side. A pair of twelve-year-old girls came by on the path. They patted the foal and then when I asked, they sang. It was Baptist and Sacred:

AMAZING GRACE

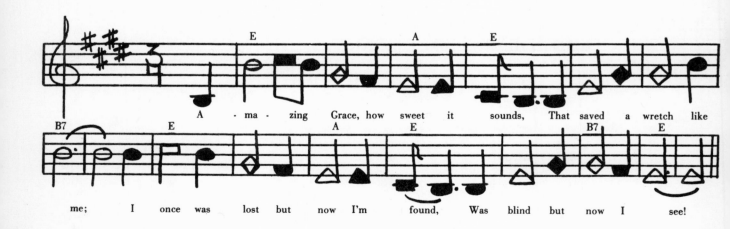

2
It was Grace that taught my heart to fear,
And Grace my fears relieved,
How precious did the Grace appear
The hour I first believed.

3

Through many dangerous toils and snares
I have already come;
It's Grace has brought me safe this far,
And Grace will lead me home!

4

How long, dear Saviour, oh how long,
Have I on earth to stay?
Roll on, roll on, ye wheels of time
And bring that joyful day!

I remembered that the Bible's sixty-seventh Psalm instructed, *Let the nations be glad and sing for joy.* The two girls, barefoot, their jet-black hair in braids, the ends tied with colored yarn, were coaxing the foal, lifting him to his feet. He stood half-sleepy, nibbling at their dress and sleeve hems. Their frocks were sleezy and handed-down; they had been bought from the racks in the ten-cents-to-a-dollar store in the nearby town. Their hair was shiny, their features even and comely, their figures slender.

They sang a religious hill tune that I'd heard Frank Warner render in our living room. My children had fastened to the balladeer, wide-eyed. He had gone up into the hills to find his songs, and accompanied them on his famous autographed wood banjo, his voice like the mountain people:

HOLD MY HAND

Hold my hand, Lord Je-sus, hold my hand, Hold my hand, Lord Je-sus, hold my hand, There's a race to be run And a vic-tory to be won, Ev-ery ho-ur, give me po-wer to go through!

2

I'm your child, Lord Jesus, I'm your child,
I'm your child, Lord Jesus, I'm your child,
There's a race to be run
And a victory to be won,
Every hour, give me power to go through!

Those who lived in the hills were solemn about their churches. I was told how some would wash each other's feet, the men kiss each other's cheeks. They wished consciously, openly, to practice their religion; they were preoccupied with it. They took their singing seriously:

LORD, BUILD ME A CABIN

Lord, build me a ca-bin in the cor-ner of glo-ry land, Un-der-neath the tree of life where it can e-ver stand. Let me hear them an-gels sing-ing, Let me shake them an-gels' hands; Lord, build me a ca-bin in the cor-ner of glo-ry land!

Sometimes when the boys brought girls to church, or when he was interested in a special girl inside, he'd stay outside and wave through the windows or call to the desired one seated within the old country church, as familiar as home to both of them. The hymnbooks the girls held were sometimes printed with "buckwheat" notes to indicate the keys of each: *do, ray, me, faw, sol, law, te, do.*

OLD HUNDRED

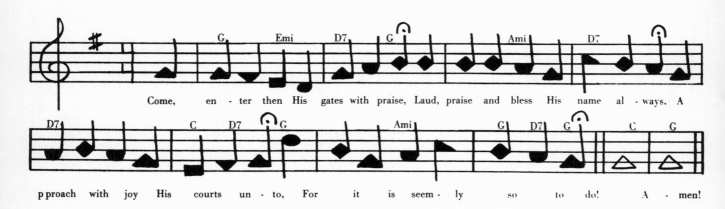

Come, en-ter then His gates with praise, Laud, praise and bless His name al-ways. Ap-proach with joy His courts un-to, For it is seem-ly so to do! A-men!

The mountain folk were aware of their stubborn nature; one spoke of his child's death in the past spring. "You couldn't make Dulcie take her medicine. She would not. She was a Stuart clear through. And no one could never make a Stuart not do a thing he didn't wish to do."

One heard the quadruple negative here, amazed. It did not harm the English tongue. I was reminded of my own child's playmate complaining, with prepositions, "Why did you bring the other book to us to be read *to out of from for?*"

They sang dancing songs dating back to their Old War and far back before that:

THE OLD CODGER

Oh, there was an old cod-ger and he had a wood-en leg; He ne-ver had to-bac-co, so to-bac-co he would beg; The o-ther old cod-ger was a sly old fox, And he al-ways had to-bac-co in his old to-bac-co box!

Some they learned in the schoolrooms:

POP! GOES THE WEASEL

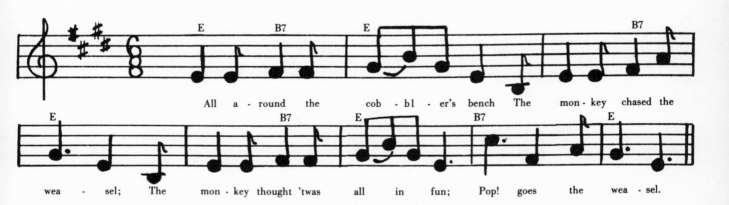

All a-round the cob-bl-er's bench The mon-key chased the wea-sel; The mon-key thought 'twas all in fun; Pop! goes the wea-sel.

They made additions where they pleased:

> Pappy's got the whooping cough;
> Mammy's got the measles;
> That's the way the money goes,
> Pop! goes the weasel.
>
> All around the American flag,
> All around the Eagle,
> The peddler kissed the preacher's wife;
> Pop! goes the weasel.

The people of the hills were free of self-consciousness about their songs. Their children learned early to take it for granted that one sang at chores and where fires were lit. One fellow, asked for a tune by a collector who'd gone rummaging about with a tape recorder and notebook, was told, "Oh, if I were only driving the cows home right now, I could sing it for you straight off."

THE CHERRY TREE

As Jo-seph and Ma-ry were walk-ing on the green, There were a-pples and cher-ries in plen-ty to be seen.

2
And Mary said to Joseph all meek and all mild,
"Please gather me some cherries for I am with child."

3
Then Joseph grew angry, all angry grew he,
"Let the daddy of the baby gather cherries for thee!"

4
And up spoke Lord Jesus from in Mary's womb,
"Bow down, you cherry tree, so my mother can have some."

5
The cherry tree bowed down, down low to the ground,
And Mary gathered her some cherries while Joseph stood around.

6
Then Joseph took Mary all on his left knee,
"For what I have done, Lord have mercy on me!"

7
Then Joseph took Mary all on his right knee,
"Pray tell me, little baby, when your birthday shall be?"

8
"On the fifth day of January my birthday shall be,
And the hills and high mountains shall kneel unto me!"

Riding upon Big Hungry Mountain one day with a hill friend, a hotel spot was pointed out to me, where the owner had run out of money, after building a twenty-story structure, planning a skyscraper there on top of the world. He'd had to tear everything down and try to get back what he could from the scrap. I was told that for a year afterwards, people had hauled away bathtubs by twos and threes.

We rode through the estates of Charleston people, whose relatives far back had used to journey to the mountains in coaches, and fill the summer mansions, high-ceilinged and pillared. The grounds were laid out like English parks, with broad sweeping lawns and ancient trees. They came out to speak with us, their accents cultivated, their faces soft, another breed from the mountaineers.

They told of ghosts who walked, near-ancestors. The relative of one not long deceased, Uncle Jemmy, did not go up and down the stairs in the twilight or the early dawn with gentle and squeaking ways. He went as in life, stamping and loud, disturbing his women. Uncle Jemmy had used to make the women come to prayers too, twice a day, in the living room. There was a marble-topped table where the Bible was throned, and by it Uncle Jemmy had sat and bent all to their knees at the proper times. They told of how when Uncle Jemmy had married his wife, they had gone slowly up the aisle, each carrying the other's gold ring upon a velvet cushion stuffed with their own parents' love-letters.

Leaving the estates on their rolling plateaus, we went up into the mountains, past the village, Upward, and came in time to Five Point Mountain. We went along a stony ox-cart road where the horses stumbled. We had come to visit a witch woman who lived in an old early-model contraption labeled *County School Bus*. It was full of cracks, had a stove, a tarpaulin over the cot, a sack for a pillow, and nearly fifteen cats. The woman's face was square, very old, puckered and dry, her eyes were violet and small. She came out to pray over us:

"Lord Jesus, come and put your arms close about these people like you do for me." She cried it out as if she spoke to a great crowd. "Dear sweet-smelling Jesus, pour your blessings on these sweet things and fill them with love. You know how I worship your works, Oh Lamb of God, and take no medicine, relying on faith. Pour out your blessing on these persons just like that other one that came a while back, a year ago, and gave me some money."

At last she let us go, and we went down the path, and then cantering on the open stretches, the colt at our side. We went by a stone cross with its message, "Get Right With God." The people were severe in their religion. They had used to deal roughly with transgression. There was a story of a sinner brought to the hanging rope. Before they drove the mule out from under him, they said, "Martin, you got ary last word you'd like to say for the people?"

And Martin got mad, truculent. "Look here," he said, "I come all this way over here to be hung, not to make conversation."

And I was back in the stable at home in time for milking. I was hanging the bridle on its peg, the saddle and blanket on the rack, and brushing down the horses. We had purchased milking machines for the goats; everything had been painted white, the animals were clipped regularly, the udders washed carefully, and we were inspected at unscheduled times. We were producing certified unpasteurized milk. I washed up and slipped into my white coat and went to the dairy house.

And at supper time I went tramping up the road to the house. There on the porch were three indignant persons: one tall and white-haired, one small and red-haired, the other small and yellow-haired.

"Mr. McGillicuddy's gone, Helga," shouted the red-head.

The yellow-head shook her head. "Someone's takened his hat!"

"Marauders have been here," the white-head reported. "They've absconded with that old hat I could stick so handy in my belt. It is, as Charles Lamb once said, definitely gonested. Not just gone, not just plain old gone. But gonested!"

And the three sighed and went away as I turned to the kitchen. I felt that some day old Michael McGillicuddy would find his way back. The trio were singing. The white-head was flipping a small open pocket-knife from the back of his hand, and the red-head having learned his lesson, was snatching three quarters nimbly before they fell:

HAND ME DOWN MY WALKING CANE

Hand me down my walk-ing cane, Hand me down my walk-ing cane, Hand me down my walk-ing cane, All don't see me gon-na hear me sing, 'bout all my sins been ta-ken way, tak-en a - way!

2
My feet got wet in the midnight dew . . .
And the morning star was a witness too,
That all my sins been taken away, taken away!

3
Don't you hear that whistle blow . . .
Take my hat and I'm gonna go,
For all my sins been taken away, taken away!

That night the moon blazed bright as day; never in my days had I known so brilliant a moon. I scuffed through the damp night grass, wandering over the rocks that sometimes lay bare in the middle of fields. Impressed, I later put them in a book, the heroine saying, "Sometimes a rock grows so big in a field they plow in a ring about it. Our hired hand claimed those rocks were nailed to the center of the world where the fire is. To hold the earth together." That had been told me by a hill man, and it could be so.

I was content with the land we had come to, remembering an old Swede joke. A Rich Man had come to a Poor Swede and told him, "I'll grant you three wishes. What do you want?" And the poor Swede thought a while. "A box of cigars, the best!" "It is yours. Next." And after a long time the Swede said, "And a bottle of wine, the best." "Now, what is your third wish?" And after much pondering the Swede finally said, "Well, I'll take another bottle of that wine."

PART FIVE

*. . . Leadbelly did not know where his guitar
would carry him, but he said that he would
follow it. His guitar was not like a friend
of his, not like a woman, not like some of
the kids, not like a man you know. But it
was a thing that would cause people to walk
over to where he is . . .*

—WOODY GUTHRIE

*. . . The guitar makes dreams weep . . . it weaves a
great star to trap sighs floating in its dark
wooden well . . .*

—FEDERICO GARCIA LORCA

And then half a dozen years after we'd come to the farm, the children and I were putting on traveling shoes again. We were going to a city. All of my life I had lived in open country, in some isolated house. We never locked doors, never knew where the keys were to fit them, lost in some drawer with other unknown keys. Nothing was ever stolen; no intruder ever came. Keys remained in the ignitions of cars, from the first Model-T to the last four-wheel-drive mountain jeep.

I was used to country ways and read the almanac regarding the light and dark of the moon, as well as subscribing to the latest scientific farm journal. Who knew what was truth and what lore? On the farm was a small herd of Black Angus beef cows, and to get them with calf we had used artificial insemination and had had fifty-fifty luck. One spring, my mother told the herdsman, "Let's let the old cow raise her bull calf this year." And in that fall he settled all the little herd, including his dam.

"Sure to God, I could have told you," the herdsman declared. "You can't beat nature."

And we were leaving the natural life. We were used to shouting and slamming doors, to a wide bowl of sky spreading uninterrupted by sharp corners. The Doberman Pinscher, Leif, was used to patrolling farm boundaries. We called him to the car and he sat in the back seat between Paula and John. There were three catcarriers on the floor, full of varied Siamese kittens and cats. The children hung out of the open back windows and I drove; it took us twelve hours to reach Washington, D.C.:

WANDERING

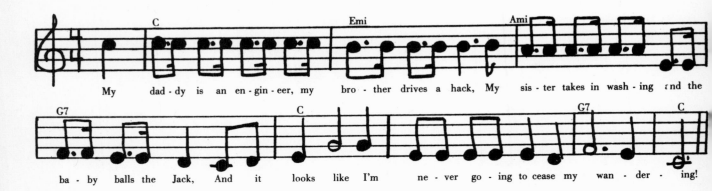

My dad-dy is an en-gin-eer, my bro-ther drives a hack, My sis-ter takes in wash-ing and the ba-by balls the Jack, And it looks like I'm ne-ver go-ing to cease my wan-der-ing!

2
I've been wandering early and late,
New York City to the Golden Gate,
And it looks like I'm never going to cease my wandering!

3
Snakes on the mountain, eels in the sea,
It took a red-headed woman to make a wreck out of me,
And it looks like I'm never going to cease my wandering!

4
Ashes to ashes and dust to dust,
If drinking don't kill you, then the women must,
And it looks like I'm never going to cease my wandering!

We took to the city easily. There was an excitement to it, a freshness, busy. After a long time I learned to be oblivious to loud noises if they didn't concern me. A Voice of America man was taping an interview in my living room and I was singing.

"Stop," he said.

"But why?" I asked, mild.

"Don't you hear the fire engines? It's spoiling the reel." Under the window the red city beasts rushed, clanging and shrieking, the rescue truck bawling. I never heard, separated from them. They were stabled a few blocks away and I was used to them at any hour.

Leif went on his rounds at the first opportunity, and in the coming years I rescued dogs of all sizes, Bulls, Terriers, Great Danes, from his white teeth and peremptory manner. He took slowly, dubious, my head-shaking and loud calling. When the Welcome Wagon lady arrived at the door as we were first unpacking, her large basket of gifts on her arm and a great garden hat on her head, I heard the throaty growl of danger, and turned to see the Doberman rising in wonder. I caught him by a hind leg as he flashed by in my defense.

"Please go quickly," I suggested, and she fled.

The postman was greeted with the same dangerous sound, and only slowly, bewildered, did the country dog come to accept his confinement and most of the new laws.

The city was lively and varied. We found Washington provincial and friendly, and quickly we got along. We heard the mockingbird, and found that it was as common as in the Carolina hills. In the city's midst was a deep ravine, a handsome forest, a wide stream, and a spreading zoological park. One could hear the lions roar when the wind blew right, and all the time the birds sang. Ages ago, a vultures' roost had been established; in the way of birds of this sort, they had managed to ignore our human presences and circled, soaring, on high, their enormous wings spread in the wind tides. The poet St. John Perse said, "They held the town under the charm of their grand manners."

The children took to the city also. I heard the yellow-haired one improvising with her friends, somewhere beyond the closed doors of my study. I listened: the tune was an old family favorite, known over the nation, "All God's Chillen Got Shoes":

> *I got gum, you got gum, all God's chillen got gum,*
> *When you get to heaven, gonna chew that gum,*
> *And pass it 'round to all the angels in heaven, heaven,*
> *Gonna chew it all over God's heaven!*

And my child's clear voice solo:

> *I got a goat, you got a goat, all God's chillen got a goat,*
> *When you get to heaven, gonna milk that goat,*
> *Give goat milk to Baby Jesus in heaven, heaven,*
> *We'll have goats all over God's heaven!*

Far into the afternoon their voices went:

YOU CAN'T GET TO HEAVEN
ON ROLLER SKATES

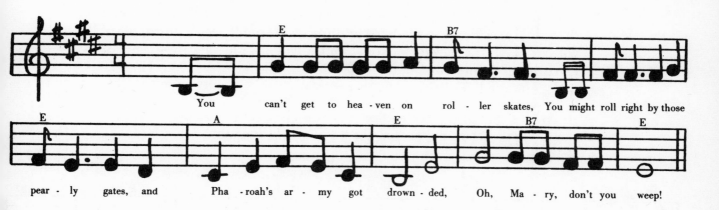

2
You can't get to heaven in Paula's car,
Because the gosh-darn thing won't go that far! . . .

137

3
You can't get to heaven in David's limousine,
Because the darn-fool thing's out of gasoline! . . .

And sometimes they were singing in lilting chorus, new tunes, considered by some to be slightly revolutionary. They were ardent:

IT COULD BE A WONDERFUL WORLD

If each lit-tle kid could have fresh milk each day, If each work-ing man had e-nough time to play, If each home-less soul had a good place to stay, It could be a won-der-ful world. If we could con-si-der each oth- er, A neigh-bor, a friend, or a bro-ther, It could be a won-der-ful, won-der-ful world, It could be a won-der-ful world!

2
If there were no poor and the rich were content,
If strangers were welcome wherever they went,
If each of us knew what true brotherhood meant,
It could be a wonderful world,

And then late one night, to my desk, from the other room, came the raised voices of the red-head and his male friends, with gusto, deep-voiced; it was a parody on our gentle tune, "The Twelve Days of Christmas." I interrupted and asked if I could put it on tape. Patient, they consented, and then I beat a retreat:

THE TWELVE DAYS OF MARXMAS

On the first day of Marx-mas my com-rades gave to me a pic-ture of Le-on Trot-

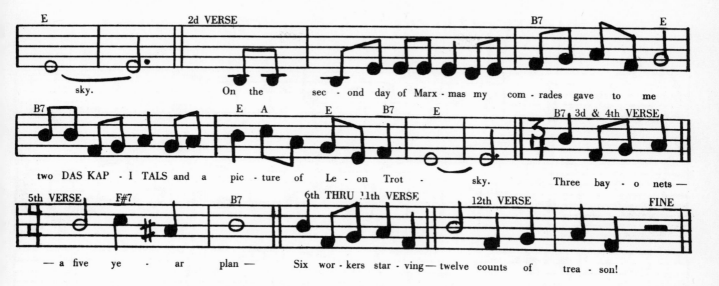

sky. On the sec-ond day of Marx-mas my com-rades gave to me two DAS KAP-I TALS and a pic-ture of Le-on Trot-sky. Three bay-o nets — — a five ye-ar plan — Six wor-kers star-ving — twelve counts of trea-son!

On the third day of Marxmas my comrades gave to me
Three bayonets, two *Das Kapitals* and a picture of Leon Trotsky.

On the fourth day of Marxmas my comrades gave to me
Four bowls of borsch . . .

On the fifth day of Marxmas my comrades gave to me
A five-year plan . . .

On the sixth day of Marxmas my comrades gave to me
Six workers starving . . .

On the seventh day of Marxmas my comrades gave to me
Seven Lenins leaping . . .

On the eighth day of Marxmas my comrades gave to me
Eight Stalins staring . . .

On the ninth day of Marxmas my comrades gave to me
Nine bloody purges . . .

On the tenth day of Marxmas my comrades gave to me
Ten sputniks spinning . . .

On the eleventh day of Marxmas my comrades gave to me
Eleven vats of Vodka, ten sputniks spinning, nine
    bloody purges, eight Stalins staring, seven Lenins
    leaping, six workers starving, a five-year plan,
    four bowls of borsch, three bayonets, two *Das
    Kapitals,* and a picture of Leon Trotsky!

On the twelfth day of Marxmas my comrades gave to me
TWELVE COUNTS OF TREASON!

When I was back at work later, I got to thinking that most people
must have favorite songs. Curious, bold, I wrote President Kennedy,
who listed an old-fashioned one:

GREENSLEEVES

A - las, my love, you do me wrong, To treat me so dis-
court - eous - ly, when I have loved you so long, de - light - ing in your
com - pan - y. Green - sleeves was my de - light, Green - sleeves was all my joy,
Green - sleeves was my heart of gold, And none but the La - dy Green - sleeves!

And I inquired of new friends. Secretary Stewart Udall said he too was old-fashioned. He had picked "Greensleeves," and another:

BLACK IS THE COLOR

But black is the col - or of my true love's hair, His face is like some rosy fair, The
pret - ti - est face and the neat - est hands, I love the ground where - on he stands.

2
The winter's passed and the leaves are green,
The time is gone that we have seen,
But yet I hope the time may come
When you and I shall be as one.

3
My own true love, so fare you well,
The time has passed, but I wish you well;
And still I hope the time may come
When you and I will be as one!

My old friend Senator Benton said his mother had played the guitar. "She sang beautifully. Her favorite for me was 'Billy Boy.'" She had taken young Bill out to west Montana with her to homestead after his father died. They filed and proved up; Bill cleared the land of rock.

BILLY BOY

Oh, where have you been, Bil-ly boy, Bil-ly boy, Oh, where have you been charm-ing Bil-ly? I have been to seek a wife for the plea-sures of my life, She's a young girl and can-not leave her mo-ther.

2
Can she bake a cherry pie, Billy boy, Billy boy,
Can she bake a cherry pie, charming Billy?
She can bake a cherry pie, quick as a cat can wink its eye,
She's a young girl and cannot leave her mother.

3
Did you ask her for to wed, Billy boy, Billy boy,
Did you ask her for to wed, charming Billy?
Yes, I asked her for to wed, and this was what she said,
"I'm a young girl and cannot leave my mother!"

And Adlai Stevenson, who has said poetically, "Nothing in this universe baffles man as much as man himself," labeled among the melodies of which he was most fond:

JEANNIE WITH THE LIGHT BROWN HAIR

I dream of Jea-nie with the light brown hair, Borne like a va-por on the sum-mer air, I see her trip-ping where the bright streams play, Hap-py as the dai-sies that dance on her way! Man-y were the wild notes her mer-ry voice would call, Ma-ny were the blithe birds that war-bled them all, I dream of Jea-nie with the light brown hair, Float-ing like a va-por on the soft sum-mer air!

I went visiting Connemara, down in North Carolina. It was Christmas; Harry Golden was there. Ralph McGill of Atlanta had sent champagne for everyone, and we stayed up singing old songs and saluting everybody from the donor McGill to Caroline Kennedy's pony. I had discovered a song not long ago, and we kept returning to it all the evening long. It was the first one I had ever known which paid respects to fertilizer and top soil and electricity.

At midnight we phoned Atlanta, and sang it over the lines. When we were done, McGill sighed, tolerant, sleepy, "Merry Christmas, farmers."

THE TVA SONG

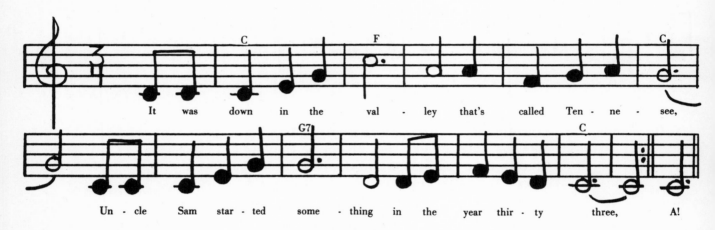

It was down in the val - ley that's called Ten - ne - see,

Un - cle Sam star - ted some - thing in the year thir - ty three, A!

2

Now rivers that once ran unchecked to the sea
Use the force that was wasted for electricity,
And rains that washed topsoil away in the night
Help turn the great turbines, turning dark into light.

3

Where once private power said it couldn't be done,
You can see farmlights twinkling, you can hear highlines hum.
Fertilizer and science are reclaiming the soil
And REA coops help to lighten the toil.

4

From the vision of Norris, who was true to a dream,
Came a blueprint for freedom and democracy's team,
The farmer and worker helped to build a new day
That was made for the people of the great U.S.A.!

And then two things happened in my life, which would change it somewhat: I went to Europe and I got a guitar. I traveled mostly under the State Department as an American Specialist. But first, initiating the trip, I had been offered a grant by the Finnish-American Society, a part of the American Scandinavian Foundation. I went through England, Sweden, Denmark, Belgium, Luxembourg, West

Germany. *Svenska Institutet,* a Swedish cultural organization, sponsored two weeks, during which time I went to Göteborg to the Hermann Carlson Levin factory where my guitar was made.

The woods were varied; if the wood of an instrument was hard and strong, so was its tone. The back and sides were of mahogany, which gave a soft tone, and was from Honduras and the Philippines; the decorations were of rosewood from Brazil; the frets of ebony from Africa; the blond wood of its face was Rumanian spruce from the German Alps. Before long I would feel strongly about my guitar; it would be a small animal, alive and waiting. I asked them to send the instrument, and a mandolin for my son, to America.

That was April; I would stay in Europe until late August. I was lecturing or conducting seminars of writers, publishers and poets. I went walking into bookstores, asking to fill my fountain pen; it was a ruse so I could stay to talk with the proprietors and clerk about the state of writing in the country, and the position of translations of their books into my language. There were press conferences and luncheons and dinners. The ambassadors were about, and at one meal, at the Swedish PEN Club, Prince William showed me how to pepper lox properly.

In Finland I saw and heard the red-bosomed Bullfinches, and sent home books in Finnish with many photographs by Yryo Kokko, their animal doctor, poet of trees and birds and little beasts. I had a strong feeling of kinship with the country. I noticed people with high cheekbones and face structures like my own. I was looking for it, having heard that the countryside in Sweden where my grandmother came from was once an old Finn colony. And my father had said he was a Black Swede.

It was easy to like the Finns, the winter-pale courteous men who laughed readily, the cordial women, and the old people in the streets with brooms and shovels and instant smiles. The coffee was kept warm with cozies and served in miniature cups. I went about amazed, feeling at home. Everywhere was a multitude of flowers, tied with reeds; there were open market places where chickens were dressed with feet and claws still on, where great stiff black eels were stacked like firewood, and huge bloodied fish gaped open-mouthed just hauled in from the nearby sea. In farmers' fields terns and gulls went plucking in furrows like domestic fowl.

And continually there was a clear light and it was harsh, and I was told it differed from the soft light of south Europe which favored women's complexions. They said too, that only painters who knew gray could copy the hills and forests where birches crowded with dark firs.

On the plane bound for Sweden, a Finn told me that a nightingale had been heard to sing already in Jyväskylä, and I realized that it was not into moonlight or darkness as our mockingbird will do in his soft liquid way, but into the blazing white sunlight of the north country.

The Finn was talkative. "I met one of your American countrymen once who said his mother had told him that he must wait for dark always to eat his supper. And so midnight drew near finally, and dusk came. He went into a restaurant. When he came out at 2:00 dawn was breaking."

"Shall I believe you?" I said.

And then we landed in Stockholm. I walked about on the old unwarmed streets, looked at St. George on his iron beast, and at a statue of Karl the Twelfth, a metal man on the grass with a sword unsheathed in a gauntleted hand, spiked chains encircling him as he pointed to the sky in the east where the palace lay, and spoke in words of stone of justice and arms and equality.

I roomed at the Reisen Hotel where shipmasters still came to eat and spend the nights. I was welcomed, to my surprise; there were flowers in my room and the clerk said precisely, "And how are your father?"

"*Tack sa mycket, bra.* Very well, thanks." I told him I'd always heard of the *gamla hemlandet,* the old country.

I knew my grandmother's mother had been a gooseherd in the countryside called *lilla Östergotland,* where I planned to visit. Our father had written of me when I was tiny:

> . . . *The north has loved her; she will be*
> *A grandmother feeding geese on frosty*
> *Mornings . . .*

From the window of the Reisen I watched the blue strand where ships approached bawling to be leashed to the wharf, to lie rocking, Sweden's flags strung from their masts. I kept remembering all the blond saints and lady-faced kings and pierced blue-eyed monsters I'd seen in one day.

My cousins and relations in *lilla Östergotland* expected me; I had thought to stumble my own way and by local inquiry find them. But I was taken to the little farm near Apuna where my Grandmother Sandburg was born. There were barns and a house, all red with white trim. In the yard old trees stood in green grass and unfamiliar birds sang. The paths were scalloped in a pattern with the rake-tines: no weed was among the flowers by the side. On a pole above wavered this country's flag. And in the lawn bloomed yellow flowers and blue ones, matching the banner's colors. They were the *Scilla,* familiar to Americans, and the yellow *Ranunculus Ficaria,* not unlike our buttercup. They repeated the colors of the flag trembling above and whispering, "Sweden," as did the yellow sun and cloudless blue.

Herr Gustavsson's wife came to me, bearing a round cake with *Helga* in scrolled spun sugar among the decorations, the first baked in my honor since I was a baby. My cousins were arriving with arms full of flowers. I saw their features like my sisters and myself, and sensed the odd new tie. They spoke little English and I appealed to my interpreter. "Tell her I say this and this!"

We were caught up in sentimentality, brought together by chance. This was my father's land, I repeated, and said I would return. In the house, coffee was set out on a linen-covered table in the low-ceilinged long room. And heavy cream and cookies: *sprits, finsk, pinne, kokoskaka, kringle;* their names were told off. The china was old, unmatched, fragile. The cakes were decorated with fruit and custards. On the scrubbed board floors were panels of rag runners. The windows were tiny and ancient, the glass wavery, the curtains starched.

We carried our plates out into the sunlight; I sat on the milk bench outside the barn door. We went later to the church where my grandmother was confirmed. The organist played a medieval hymn, *Den Blomstertid Nu Kommer,* "The Time of the Flowers Has Come." And then to see other cousins who had prepared a country meal of Swedish dishes, served by the hostess of the household in the American Midwest country way, refusing to sit, preferring to tend her guests.

I knew a song in their language, and they sang it with me, pleased. It was a blessing:

HOSIANA

Pris och ä-ra sjun-ga vi, Her-ren Je-sus som köpt oss fri;
ho-si-a-na, ho-si-an-na, ho-si-a-na, sjun-ga vi Gud namm!

> We praise Lord Jesus gratefully,
> Who gave Himself to make us free;
> Halleluia, halleluia, halleluia,
> We sing God's name!

The children in the house wrote in my journal something for me to remember:

> *Pa gamla dar, när synen sviker dig,*
> *Tag brillor pa och läs och tänk pa mig!*

which I translated slowly:

> *When you are old and cannot see,*
> *Put on your specs and think of me!*

We drove back to the village of Motala, where I was staying. It had been a long winter. Swedes are sun-worshipers, as I knew, and they had lined up along walls, eyes shut, heads bent up to the rays.

A butterfly drifted past, bright yellow, and my interpreter said, "Your cousin says that you can tell the kind of summer coming by the first butterfly. If it is light colored, it will be sunny."

I nodded, catching his pale blue eyes that were like my own. "I have heard the same thing in Michigan in my country. It is good luck." I felt at home.

I went wandering all over south Sweden, to the farm country of Smäland, down to Mälmo, to Göteborg, up to Marstrand and its castle and sea. Always I returned to Stockholm where my embassy friends were and other new friends. I filled my journals. I sang, for the writer Vilgot Sjöman, folk songs which I found already popular there. Vilgot wanted to know all the words. We sat in a restaurant on the top of the town:

WAILIE WAILIE

When co-ckle she-ll-s turn sil-ver be-ll-s, Then will my love re-turn to me, Oh, wai-lie, wai lie! But love is bon-nie A lit-tle while when it is new!

The Swedes and the Finns taught me to skal, and I decided to speak to my son of it when I returned. They saluted:

> *Min skal, din skal,*
> *Alla vackra flickors skal!*
> I *skal* you, myself,
> And all the beautiful women!

The rest of my time in Europe I was on my own, incognito. I found that Olga or Elga, and *Santamontagna* or *Montagna di Sabbia*, was as close as the natives would come. I traveled as low a class as possible. "Don't they have steerage?" I demanded, "because my grandmother came over that way."

"Long ago, that was done away with. Yes."

"Well."

I filled seven notebooks. "Always she is writing," my new acquaintances said.

I was roaring down into Switzerland in an overcrowded coach, perched on my luggage in the narrow passageway, hanging out of the open window, staring, humming. I stayed in Italy for a couple of weeks, sent an Italian guitar, a Monzino, to my classic-minded son, now twenty. Then I boarded a small ship for Greece, to stay a few days.

It was August. I took the tour to Adelphi, and was in a rumbling bus for thirteen hours. The trip was commanded by an English-speaking woman for whom I developed strong hostile emotions. She was dubbed The General.

"I will not do as she says," I growled to a fellow passenger, a Frenchman.

"Then you will not see all the ruins."

"*Oui?*"

And he laughed, "I understand."

When I arrived back at my pension on our return at dark, I said firmly to the concierge. "I wish to cancel all the 'See Greece with Me' trips I signed up for."

"Impossible."

"I am going to spend my time at the Acropolis up there, and swimming at Asteria on the sea."

His eye did not meet mine. He was combing his mustache with a tender movement, gazing in a tiny hand mirror. "It cannot be done. *Óhi.* No."

"I haven't paid my money yet."

"That is true." He put his comb aside and glanced at me. "Very well. Now, will you have a beer with me before you go to your room?"

"If you will translate your newspaper for me, please." I had seen a picture of Hemingway. "Tell me of this."

"That man, did you know, Hemingwood, is dead. It says he did the book '*Goodbye to the Guns*' and '*The Bells Are Ringing.*'"

"Oh!" It was far away.

I went out in the evenings to drink the coffee in the open street cafés where tables were set up before an open-air stage. In the afternoons I swam at the beaches outside Athens, sometimes giving my billfold and watch to an old Greek woman who put them in her pocket and on her wrist to guard them.

"Count your money," said my friend.

"*Óhi.* I do not count my money to her." I felt her firm honesty; her white teeth flashed as he translated what I'd said.

I swam to the raft and stayed there. "How do you say *pesce, Signora?*" an Italian asked.

"We say fish."

"*Si.* You are a fish."

And then I was on a little Mediterranean boat bound for Nice. It was a three-day journey to France. There was a Corsican on board, traveling with a small troupe. He played a very good amplified guitar. He was dark and nervous, had long fingers and glinting teeth. And on his arm was tattooed a poniard.

"What is that?" I asked.

"The vendetta," he nodded. "When I am a young man, I am no good. *Pas bon!*"

"Well."

"You Sviss," he asked, "*Si?*"

"No."

"You *Suede,* I think?"

"American," I sighed.

"Ah. Then perhaps you know an Italian countryman of mine, name of Verrini, came once to London to teach the *chittara* to *Signore* Charles Dickens."

"No," I said politely. "That was a long time ago."

"And *Signore* Abraham Lincoln, your king. How is he?" The Corsican leaned against the rail and admired the blue water.

I was startled. "All right, I guess."

"About America, I know many things. I have read this. Now, if you will bring your friends to our cabin I will play for you the American music. Since we are the professionals, it is not *permisse* for us to play in the lounge." He ran his finger across his swarthy throat. "The Union."

"*Gracias,*" I breathed.

I expected something like "St. Louis Blues" or "Take Me For a Buggy Ride," both of which I'd heard in Bonn, and in Oulu, Finland, just below the Arctic Circle, and in Rome. But in a strange beat the Italian rendered one of our ballads, one I'd learned from my sister Margaret at a tender age. In it the *Good,* Sweet William, died of love and red roses sprang from him. And the *Cruel,* Barbry Ellen, followed him to the grave, done in by sorrow. And the briars that grew, united in time with the flowers. Such was the ballad's law.

The Corsican tuned his guitar:

BARBRY ELLEN

In Scar - let Town where I come from, There was a fair maid dwel - ling, made ev - ery youth cry, "Well a - way!" and her name was Bar - bry El - len!

2
It was in the merry month of May
When the green buds were swelling,
Sweet William on the death bed lay
For the love of Barbry Ellen.

3
And death was written on his face,
And on his heart was stealing,
Make haste, make haste, to comfort him,
Oh, lovely Barbry Ellen.

4
His servant came unto her door,
To the place where she was dwelling,
Saying, "You must come to my master dear,
If your name be Barbry Ellen!"

5
And slowly slowly came she there,
And slowly came she nigh him,
And all she said when there she came,
Was, "Young man, I think you're dying!

6
"Do you recall the other day
When you were all a-drinking?
You passed the glass to the ladies all,
But you slighted Barbry Ellen!"

7
He turned his face unto the wall,
And death was with him dealing,
Says, *"Adieu, adieu,* to my kind friends all,
And adieu to Barbry Ellen!"

8
As she was going over the field
She spied his corpse a-coming,
Says, "Lay down, lay down, his corpse, my dears,
That I may look upon him."

9
She turned to the east, she turned to the west
She heard the death-bells ringing,
And every note did seem to say,
"Hard-hearted Barbry Ellen!"

10
When he was dead and put in grave,
Her heart was struck with sorrow.
"Oh, Mother, Mother, make the bed,
For I must die tomorrow."

11
And, "Father, Father, dig the grave,
And dig it deep and narrow.
Sweet William died for me this day,
I'll die for him tomorrow."

12
They buried Sweet William in the old church yard,
And Barbry Ellen beside him,
And from out of his grave sprung a red red rose
And outen hers a briar.

13
Which climbed and climbed to the old church top
Till they couldn't climb no higher;
And then they twined in a true lover's knot,
The rose about the briar!

The Corsican grinned whitely. "Is *bella,* no? You like?"
    "Si," everyone said. *"Multa bella!"*
    "And now you will sing something," he told me.

"I can't remember anything."
"An American song."
I felt the challenge. "There's an old one about Lincoln":

OLD ABE LINCOLN

Old Abe Lin-coln came out of the wil-der-ness, Out of the wil-der-ness, out of the wil-der-ness, Down in Ill-i-nois!

He accompanied me in tinkling odd jazz. *"Bene,"* he said. "I like
you Americans."
I remembered one my children had sung, and he beat it out:

THE WORLD OF TOMORROW

The world of to-mor-row they tell me will be a world where all peo-ple are ha-py and free, So if you hate war I am sure you will say, Let's make the world of to-mor-row to-day!

2
Tomorrow the world will grow plenty of wheat
And plenty of food for the hungry to eat,
But if you are hungry I'm sure you will say,
Let's make the world of tomorrow today.

3
The world of tomorrow we'll borrow and lend,
We'll help one another like neighbor and friend,
Tomorrow, tomorrow seems so far away,
Let's make the world of tomorrow today!

And as we left, I told him, dogged, "We have a president now.
We don't have kings!"
"So?" he smiled, cradling the huge wood thing. "Then you will
give my respects to *Presidente* Lincoln, *por favor*, at the *casabianca*."

150

I shrugged. "All right."

"Va bene."

"Go well."

And we were disembarking at Nice. Lazy, I took a train to Cannes, and revoked my plans to go up through *Provence* on a literary tour. The French railroad officials said it was impossible ever to change tickets. They were upset and shouted and waved, and I began to laugh. Only by a miracle, my American Express man assured me later, was he able to persuade the officials. I didn't care what kind of trouble he was having.

I was standing on a diving platform twenty feet above the sea. Below, the Mediterranean churned in a *mistral* that had started, and I thought how no one anywhere knew where I was or who. The woman who rented me the tiny inside windowless room for ten old francs, was keeping my passport and billfold.

"Madeleine is honest," I had been told by a Frenchwoman who recommended the pension on the train to Cannes, "and you must leave your money and papers with her whenever you go out." I gazed into the sea and at the clouding sky and dived, content.

After a week I was on the coach train rushing up through France. I spoke enough of the language, in the present tense, to get on without English.

"It is better," Frenchmen had told me, amiable, "for you to speak the French. Our English you could never understand. Bad French we comprehend."

And soon I was on the Channel ferry, having English tea on white linen. And back in London, I went to lecture at Oxford in damaged idiom.

I remembered Lord Chesterton had written, "A patriot is someone who is always sad." I told them this, and sang them two songs about one of our great cities. A stranger, I insisted upon my loyalties; both tunes were popular in my home:

NEW YORK I

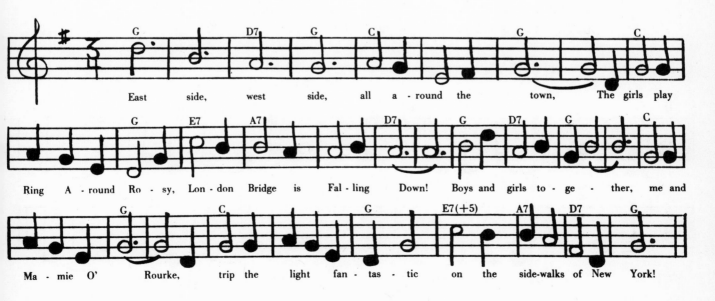

East side, west side, all a-round the town, The girls play Ring A-round Ro-sy, Lon-don Bridge is Fal-ling Down! Boys and girls to-ge-ther, me and Ma-mie O' Rourke, trip the light fan-tas-tic on the side-walks of New York!

NEW YORK II

On Broad-way, in the Bow - ry, he ram-bled up and down, On odd-ways and by - ways, re - solved to see the town, And

as he went he sang this song, "Now is - n't it a pi - ty that I should stay a-way so long from such a char-ming ci - ty?"

New York, New York, Oh, what a char - ming ci - ty, New York, New York, Oh, what a char - ming ci - ty!"

"Here Freedom, here Duty, here Truth and Joy remain,
Here Honor and Beauty, here Love and Valor reign."
And as he went he sang this song, "Now isn't it a pity,
That I should stay away so long, from such a charming city?"
CHORUS

During the months of the trip I picked up oil and water-color paintings by contemporaries, which cost relatively little. Being an amateur painter, I found it was a means of communication. I'd never been further west than Chicago, or further south than North Carolina. The shock of the Finnish tongue brought me to buying my first oil there. Then I kept it up. In every country, I listened to the songs, half understanding, often captured by the rhythm. In Stockholm and then Denmark, and later through Europe, I heard a captivating folk melody. The Swedish words were catchy. The homecoming ship band played it, and since I've heard it now and then in American night spots:

SJOMAN

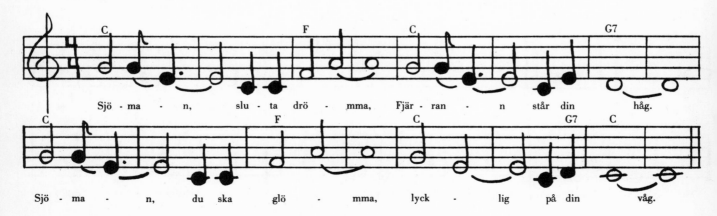

Sjö - ma - n, slu - ta drö - mma, Fjär - ran - n står din håg.

Sjö - ma - n, du ska glö - mma, lyck - lig på din våg.

Sjöman, sluta drömma, Tänk ej mer pa mej!
Sjöman, Vilda strömmar, ropar efter dej.

Sailor, stop your dreaming! Go where you must go,
Sailor, think not of me; follow winds that blow.

I lingered getting off the ship in New York. "Don't you want to go up on deck and take photographs?"

"Aren't you glad to be home!"

"In some ways." I looked forward to my guitar, which had preceded me. All my life I'd sung the songs, and for the first time I would accompany them.

I got in the New York taxicab, and started to write the address for the driver, and realized, "I speak your language!"

In another day, I was driving by the white buildings of my home town again, and the Washington cab driver told me, "Washington is the most beautiful city in the world!"

"It is true," I said, wondering if he knew how often I'd heard his phrase. "Athens is the most beautiful city in the world." "My *Napoli Belissima.*" "Paris." "Stockholm is the most fair city anywhere." "Helsinki. Copenhagen. Ah, I love London Town!"

And before a week was out I was beginning guitar lessons. My son had been practicing on his Monzino when I arrived at home. "You hear that?" he said with mathematical joy, striking the A-string, "that's four hundred and forty cycles per second!"

"It's nice to be back," I said, and went to the phone to call his teacher for my first lesson.

Born a Greek, Sophocles Papas is a modest man, student and friend of *Don* Andres Segovia. Once when I stood my instrument on the wood floor against a table, he snatched it up, hurt, paternal. "Don't do that," he sighed, and stood it on the soft rug.

I knew how the guitar was alive for the teacher. I remembered that the head of our house, when a boy, during Hard Times, had got a two-dollar banjo and learned chords from a school friend. He had written a poem to the guitar, naming it a "chattel with a soul often in part owning its owner and tantalizing him with his lack of perfection. An instrument of quaint form . . . a box of chosen wood . . . a portable companion . . . a small friend weighing less than a newborn infant."

One of Sophocles' famous pupils was Charlie Byrd, who had eleven guitars. He said he was attached to all and was never somehow able to sell one; rarely he gave one away. When I first went to watch him handling his jazz amplified instrument like an unruly horse, I felt the stir of needing to play the guitar. Ginnie Byrd sang jazz engagingly to her husband's guitar, Keter Bett's bass, and a set of drums: "Baltimore Oriole," "Don't Explain," "I Am Just a Little Girl."

And Charlie himself, the city's acknowledged master of the night guitar, rendered Bach and Sor with intrepidity, and then, with the gypsy flare of a Django Reinhart, jazz tunes. And he took old-time songs too, and played them with his trio in different rhythms. Some he gave an ancient Eastern Indian flavor, and one of these was a class-war union song, sprung from miners who used a Mountain Baptist hymn tune.

> Go lay the Lily low, go lay the Lily low!
> Go lay the Lily low, go lay the Lily low!

The coal-mining men had sung:

WHICH SIDE ARE YOU ON?

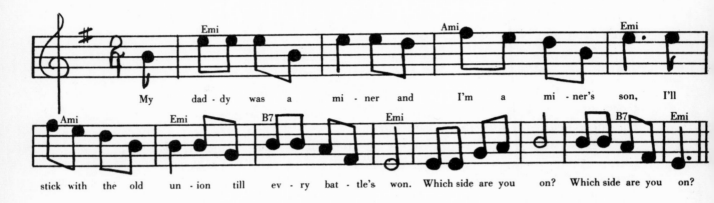

My dad-dy was a mi-ner and I'm a mi-ner's son, I'll stick with the old un-ion till ev-ry bat-tle's won. Which side are you on? Which side are you on?

After a couple of months of classic guitar lessons under Sophocles, I gave it up in order to spend time on chords and the rough country music which appealed to me. I was meeting new friends. One guitarist was Joe Glazer, a composer of songs that were sung by crowds of thousands in union hall meetings or campaign rallies. I was caught by his vivid style.

Once he was listening to a speech in which mine mules were mentioned. The animals were kept healthy even in slack times, but the miners got no attention. "And you know why, folks?" said the orator, "because it cost fifty bucks to buy another mule, but they always could get another coal miner for nothing!"

And so Joe wrote a new song:

TOO OLD TO WORK

You work in the fac-to-ry all of your life, try to pro-vide for your kids and your wife, when you get too old to pro-duce an-y more, they hand you your hat and they show you the door.

CHORUS

Too old to work, too old to work, when you're too old to work and you're too young to die,

who'-ll take care of you, how'll you get by, when you're too old to work and you're too young to die?

2

You don't ask for favors when your life is through,
You've got a right to what's coming to you,
Your boss gets a pension when he is too old,
You helped him retire, you're out in the cold!

3

They put horses to pasture, they feed them on hay,
Even machines get retired some day,
The bosses get pensions when their days are through,
Fat pensions for them, brother, nothing for you.

Joe told me he was out walking and stepped into a union meeting. He heard the announcer saying, "Let's have that old folk song, 'The Mill Was Made of Marble'!" Joe didn't tell them but some years before a textile mill had gone on strike and an old worker had written down on a scrap of paper some lines, containing the title phrase; the paper was turned over to Joe who reworked it and set it to music:

THE MILL WAS MADE OF MARBLE

I dreamed that I had di - ed, and gone to my re - ward, A job in

Hea - ven's tex - tile plant on a gol - den bou - le - vard. And the mill was made of mar - ble, the ma-

chines were made out of gold, And no - bo - dy ev - er got ti - red, and no - bo - dy ev - er grew old!

2

It was quiet and peaceful in heaven, there was no clatter or boom,
You could hear the most beautiful music as you worked at the spindle
or loom.

3

There was no unemployment in heaven, we worked steady all through
the year,
We always had food for the children; we never were haunted by fear.

4

When I woke from this dream about heaven, I wondered if someday
there'd be
A mill like that one down below here on earth, for workers like you
and like me!

Joe had begun with a Sears, Roebuck guitar when young; he
showed me the *capo* or *cejillia,* which was clasped about the strings, and
when moved up or down a fret, to lengthen or shorten the stringboard,
changed the key half a note. Joe used the honest slang term *cheater,*
which I adopted. Sophocles told me, "It is easier to learn the chord than
to move the *capo!*"

"No," I disagreed, "I am a beginner and the *cheater* is my friend."
It expanded the range without the weeks of work I needed to under-
take in the future to understand and learn all the chords.

"Have you no pride?" Sophocles asked.

"I have put vanity aside," I told him, showing him the close-filed
nails on my left fingers, and the new calluses building.

I learned that in guitar-playing as in most art, it was style that
counted. The most accomplished technician could be a bore, without
style. A natural like Woody Guthrie, who worked out his own way,
kept people on edge. He said, "I learned all I know by watching and
never could tell you what the letter and the number was anyhow."

I met all the guitarists that I could. The great one, *Don* Andres
Segovia, came, white-maned, spectacled, majestic. He shook his head
over the popular guitar-players using their picks and metal strings and
electronic amplification. "Let us say we are on opposite sides of a hill.
Who knows? Maybe we will meet some day at the top."

Montoya arrived and dazzled, completing his program with an
interpretation of "St. Louis Blues" that had the audience on their
feet. Later he cautioned young ambitious guitarists who crowded in a
circle, "You think you play very well in your room, don't you? *Ex-
cellente. Buena.* When you go upon the stage you will play exactly
one-half as well. Therefore one must play perfectly to start with."

When Olga Coelho came I asked her to use my guitar. Superstitious, I felt the instrument would profit from handling by maestros.
"I weel try," she consented, as though of some small living thing, "I
weel see if she weel respond." And after rendering a number of her
native Brazilian ballads, she turned with her brilliant smile, "I weel
seeng now for you a song of your country." It was Stephen Foster, new
and flawless:

UNDER THE WILLOW SHE'S SLEEPING

"Un - der the wil - low she's laid with care," Sang a lone mo - ther while weep - ing,

"Un - der the wil - low, with gol - den hair, My lit - tle one's qui - et - ly sleep - ing! "Fair, fair, and gol - den hair,"

Sang a lone mo - ther while weep - ing, "Fair, fair, and gol - den hair, Un - der the wil - low she's sleep - ing!"

2
"Under the willow no songs are heard,
Near where my darling lies dreaming,
Naught but the voice of some far-off bird,
Where life and its pleasures are beaming!"

I began noticing the instrumentalists who were around; Steve Jordan over in a Georgetown café beating his "rhythm" guitar in a jazz like the thirties:

> *Your dizzy walk, your dopey talk,*
> *I go for that!*

I asked Virgil Sturgil to come over from Baltimore. He brought two dulcimers and once in a while used a pigeon quill on them that he'd just picked up in the park, since there were no turkeys about the city. He had the instrument across his knees and stroked the strings with his right hand, and his left moved rather absently to make the chords. He sang for hours like a poet of olden days, in no hurry, in his own fashion. His audience never moved.

"The people in the Ozarks," he told me, "never knew one note from another. They learned from someone else's singing. Now on this dulcimer I've been playing for fifteen years, I know only D and A and D!"

It was an old-time hymn, very like I'd heard my North Carolina friends sing:

GOLDEN BELLS

There's a land be-yond the ri-ver that they call the sweet for-ev-er and you'll
One by one we'll gain the por-tals, there to dwell with the im-mor-tals ring

on-ly reach that shore by faith's de-cree. Ring those gol-den bells for you and me.

Don't you hear those bells a-ringing,
Don't you hear the angels singing?
And it's glory halleluiah, jubilee!
In that far-off sweet forever
Just beyond the silent river,
Where they'll ring those golden bells for you and me.

As he left he asked, "If you ever go by some turkeys out in the country, would you mind to pick up a few feathers for me? A turkey quill's strong, and beats a pigeon quill for strumming by a long way." I said I would.

The country was always being stirred by change; the scene was shifting continually, kaleidoscopic; the landscape was always new. This turmoil was reflected in the songs. There was the ancient Minority Problem. A taxi driver told me he'd had a Congressman for a fare, who'd told him that in a couple of thousand years we'd all look alike. I protested, "I don't want to be like you or anybody. I want to be different from everybody on earth!" Amiable, the driver agreed with me as he had with the eccentric Congressman.

I grew up to the riddle, "What's dumber than a dumb Irishman?" "A smart Swede." That was me.

And I knew about the Negro woman rushing up to the white preacher to shake his hand with animation, "Brother, your skin may be white, but when it comes to preaching, you've got a real black heart!"

In Chicago they made jokes about the new change in the relation-ships of Black and White. Once there were great race riots there, blood-shed and terror. And now about the University, where it wasn't safe to go out after dark because of the knifings, so they said, the people told each other, "It's not race against race any more. It's black and white, side by side, against the lower classes."

The turmoil was obvious in all areas. The poet Anthony Ostroff told of being impressed by his six-year-old, who had been practicing carols the night before the last day of school, *"Tannenbaum, O, Tannenbaum!"* And Tony says, "We heard him singing an innocent (oh, innocent!) revision as he marched off the next morning, "Atom bomb, O, Atom bomb!"

I went down to visit my family, and they told me that Earl Robinson had stopped by Connemara. They were taken with his songs, especially one. My sister taught it to me at once; my mother liked the last verse the best. I made the song my own; one night I sang it for the Russian Ambassador Dobrynin and my friend, Robert Frost:

BLACK AND WHITE

The ink is black, the page is white, to-ge-ther we learn to read and write, To read and write. And now a child can un-der-stand, This is the law of all the land, All the land! The ink is black, the page is white, To-ge-ther we learn to read and write, To read and write!

2
Their robes were black, their heads were white,
The schoolhouse doors were closed up tight,
Were closed up tight.
Nine judges all set down their names
To end the years and years of shame,
Years of shame!
The robes were black, the heads were white,
[WHISTLE]!

3
The slate is black, the chalk is white,
The words stand out so clear and bright,
So clear and bright.
And now at last we plainly see
The alphabet of liberty,
Liberty!
The slate is black, the chalk is white,
[WHISTLE]!

4

A child is black, a child is white,
The whole world looks upon the sight,
A beautiful sight.
For very well the whole world knows,
This is the way that freedom grows,
Freedom grows!
A child is black, a child is white,
Together we learn to read and write,
To read and write.

5

The world is black, the world is white,
It turns by day and then by night,
It turns by night.
It turns so each and every one,
Can take his station in the sun,
In the sun!
The world is black, the world is white,
[WHISTLE]!

Great militant songs rose out of America, with a swinging rhythm.
Some were heard recently among Freedom Riders. Leadbelly wrote a
hammer song:

TAKE THIS HAMMER

Take this ha - mmer, ca'y it to the cap - tain, Take this ha - mmer ca'y it to the cap - tain, Take this ha - mmer, ca'y it to the cap - tain, Tell him I'm gone, ho - ney, say I'm gone!

2

If he asks you, was I running . . .
Tell him I was flying, babe, say I was flying!

3

If he asks you, was I laughing . . .
Tell him I was crying, honey, say I was crying!

And one we'd used when I was a child, which was originally sung
by Negro regiments, patriotic, during the Civil War. Then again after
a race riot in Atlanta, fifty years ago, when they strode down the main
street by the thousands, fervent, united, impressive. The song, hypnotic,
stirred and made one turn to reading the words of old leaders; Mr.
Thomas Jefferson stating, "All authority belongs to the people!"

OH FREEDOM

Oh free-dom, oh free-dom, oh free-dom, Lord for me! And be-fore I'll be a slave, I'll be bur-ied in my grave, And go ho-me to my Lord and be free.

No more moaning, no more moaning, no more moaning! . . .
No more weeping . . .
No more starving . . .

Everywhere I was hearing the modern ballads, written by my contemporaries. They celebrated a happening, personal, political, social, or whatever. They were written in love, in hate, to point out a wrong or recount an event.

There were sweet ones about war's ending, referring to an old hope of mankind:

LAST NIGHT I HAD THE STRANGEST DREAM

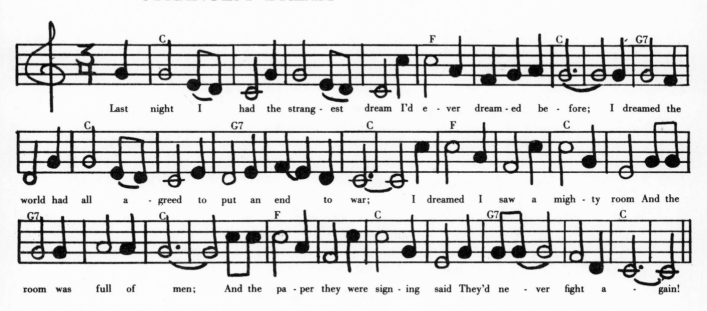

Last night I had the strang-est dream I'd e-ver dream-ed be-fore; I dreamed the world had all a-greed to put an end to war; I dreamed I saw a migh-ty room And the room was full of men; And the pa-per they were sign-ing said They'd ne-ver fight a-gain!

2
And when the paper was all signed,
And a million copies made,
They all joined hands and bowed their heads
And grateful prayers were prayed.
And the people in the streets below
Were dancing round and round,
While swords and guns and uniforms
Were scattered on the ground!

Joe Glazer sang a homemade ballad of his, in a cultured British accent, about a problem we had had here in my town; it was historical. "Who let all these foreigners in?" Glazer cried in the middle of a song. "Sandburg? Is that a foreign name!"

A TERRIBLY PRIVATE CLUB

Oh, I be-long to a pri-vate club, A ter-rib-ly, ter-rib-ly pri-vate club, Oh, I be-long to a pri-vate club in Wash-ing-ton, D. C.

2

We don't take coloreds, we don't take Jews,
We're terribly careful who we choose
To associate with in this private club in Washington, D.C.

3

If you are Catholic or Orthodox Greek,
Don't apply; you'll feel like a freak;
You wouldn't fit in this private club in Washington, D.C.

4

You may have descended from dukes or counts,
But your application we'll have to denounce
If your name is strange and hard to pronounce in Washington, D.C.

5

We just can't stand variety,
It complicates society,
This club is boring, there's no denying,
But it's also terribly satisfying
To know that the membership consists exclusively of me!
Nobody else but me! Pure American me!

I hadn't had my guitar a month when almost without knowing it I was putting down a song too, and trying it out on my indulgent friends. They quoted Tom Lehrer and Bernard Shaw to me. The former said, "The reason most folk songs are so atrocious is that they are written by the people." And the latter, "Hell is filled with musical amateurs!"

There had been a historic occurrence in my city that stunned me. Our Washington streetcars were taken away from us. When it first happened, and the mid-street ramps were chopped away, people were seen standing in herds on corners, milling. The company had to send cars around with public address systems, calling out where the new bus-stop signs were located. I was among the bewildered.

I hurried to my guitar:

THE STREETCAR SONG

'Twas in the town of Wash-ing-ton In the win-ter of six-ty-one, That the street-cars were a-bol-ished, And bus-ses be-gan to run; Gone is the bell that jin-gled, Gone the rat-tle and roar, Oh God, I wish we'd ne-ver left The age of the old street-car!

2

Where once we mounted proudly,
Now we leap and fly,
Where once we descended with dignity,
Now we stumble and sigh,
The Capital Transit System
Has made us lesser men,
Oh Lord, I wish they'd never signed
Our city's streetcars' end!

3

Oh, it's now we've crossed Dupont Circle,
And homeward we are bound,
Weaving through surface traffic,
Not roaring underground,
Go home to your wives and sweethearts,
Tell others not to come,
For the city's forsaken the streetcar tracks,
And only buses run!

One day I was in the airport setting off for Chicago, and saw in the paper that a Washington bookseller had got himself into trouble. I walked into their shop in the arcade and told his wife, "Maybe I'll write a song about this."

She flushed. "Thanks."

On the plane there was rough weather; we jerked about like a kite on a string. The Polish woman beside me said she'd been to the Russian Embassy to see if they'd let her visit her sister in Poland who was ill. "They named me a spy," she said. I didn't look at her. She began to tell over her rosary. After a while she turned to me, as the plane pitched about. "I'm not just saying these beads for myself; it's for everybody on this plane! I believe." I thanked her. She was taking care of us, the pilot was working the instruments, I was writing my song.

I knew my Jefferson, "I am mortified to be told that in the United States of America, the sale of a book can become a subject of inquiry, and of criminal inquiry too!"

BALLAD OF SAM YUDKIN

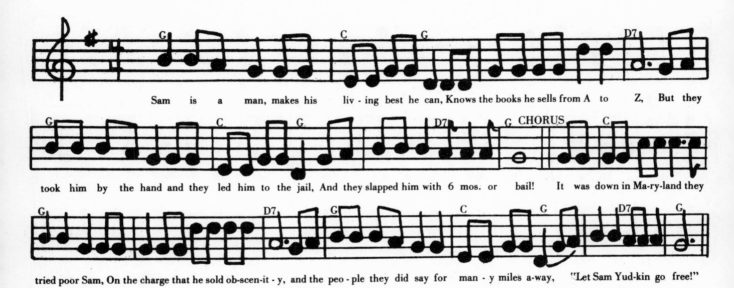

Sam is a man, makes his liv-ing best he can, Knows the books he sells from A to Z, But they

took him by the hand and they led him to the jail, And they slapped him with 6 mos. or bail! It was down in Ma-ry-land they

tried poor Sam, On the charge that he sold ob-scen-it - y, and the peo - ple they did say for man - y miles a-way, "Let Sam Yud-kin go free!"

2
How the people held their breath when they heard of Sam's arrest,
And they gathered to hear him tried.
The judge says, "Takes us common men to know what's dirtiest!"
And, "If that's literature I'll eat it," the prosecutor cried.

3
Henry wrote his *Tropics* and they caused a lot of grief,
Caused booksellers lots of woe,
They called Sam corrupting and worse than a thief,
But they better let him go!
[SPOKEN: Katherine Anne Porter says they better.
Jack Salamanca says they better.
People everywhere who believe in freedom say they better
Drop the charge: it's unconstitutional!]

And I went visiting the farm where our mother had been making top records for milk production with her dairy goat herd. I carried my guitar along to practice. Ruthless, my mother or sisters would interrupt.

"The magnolia is blooming," said one.

"There's a goldfinch at the feeding stand with the flock of purple finches," cried another.

"Here is a newborn kid!" declared the third.

"Come!" they insisted.

I thought I would prepare for them, and next time they did that, I'd sing a song. It worked; they stayed and listened. It was for Puritan Jon's Jennifer II, a nine-star milker, who had at four years of age, in 305 days, given 5750 pounds of milk, containing 191 pounds of butterfat. She was Production Champion of all the breeds of dairy goats in our country, and in all the world for all I knew! She and her whole family had received stars and cups and plaques and ribbons galore. Now she had a song too, made in honor:

JENNIFER

I want to sing you a song about the goat, Jennifer, Who gave 5 thousand seven fifty pounds in a year, For the Toggenburg breed a world record she set, and she's Mrs. Carl Sandburg's favorite pet!

CHORUS

Jennifer! mildest eyes of amber, Jennifer, softest coat of brown, Tiny ears and perfect dairy conformation, she's the sweetest little goat on Connemara Farm!

2
I want to sing you some more about the goat, Jennifer,
Whose double grandfather was Old Bolivar.
When he lowered his head the hired men would duck,
But among goatbreeders he's a three-star buck!

One day I noticed a trouble in the voice of one of my friends. I heard it the next week in another friend's. The following week I bought a *Wall Street Journal* and the song wrote itself:

BRING BACK MY MARKET

What's wrong with the In-dus-tri-al's ave—rage? What hap-pened to Dow-Jones in May? Stocks dai-ly plunge sharp-ly to new lows, Where's S and Poor's In-dex to-day? Po-lar-oid, Camp-bell's Soup, Un-i-le-ver, Lig-gett and My — oh my! high!
Poor old Ford Mo-tors, Oh bring back just one lit-tle

2
Last night as I lay on my pillow,
Last night as I lay on my bed,
I dreamed of the days of December
When most of my stocks were ahead.

3
The day was faced with *Journal* in hand,
And a modest air of prosperity,
Gently smiling,
Bring back that safe feeling to me!

4
IBM was everyone's darling,
We all adored A Tel and Tel,
I'm trying to remember not to worry,
'Cause Jack says that all will be well.

5
Trading's wild on Wall Street,
But I'm afraid to buy or to sell, oh well!
I always got *F* in Economics,
Please bring back my Bethlehem Steel!

6
Last night as I lay on my pillow,
Last night as I lay on my bed,
I suddenly woke from a nightmare,
In which my stock market dropped dead.

7
But I dreamed it, I dreamed it,
The market's alive as can be, you can see!
And I want it *bull*, and closing sky high,
Oh, bring back my market to me!

Realizing that songs must celebrate people as well as events, I wrote one for a good friend who was having a birthday. I sang it for him in his kitchen while the cook set out baked beans and sausages and pickled beets, and he poured a huge strong tumbler of tea for himself, and a kitchen glass of Manischewitz sweet wine for me. He liked the present:

BIRTHDAY SONG

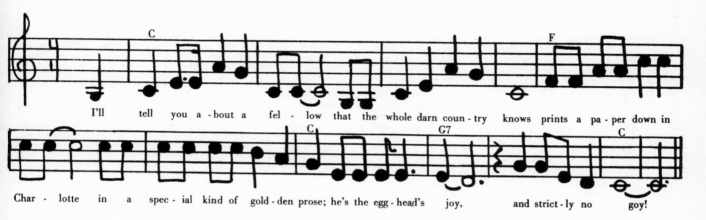

I'll tell you a-bout a fel-low that the whole darn coun-try knows prints a pa-per down in

Char-lotte in a spec-ial kind of gold-den prose; he's the egg-head's joy, and strict-ly no goy!

2
He's always pitching into issues,
Big and little, here and there,
He waves his arms and grins his grin,
And bites down on his long cigar;
He's the teen-agers' joy, America's boy!

3
You walk up to a taxi,
You're in a hurry to get somewhere,
And the driver says, "Please don't bother me,
I'm reading *Only In America!*"
Who is this man the people understand?

4
You go into a café,
And you order a plate of chow mein,
The waitress says, "Please don't bother me,
I'm reading *For 2 Cents Plain!*"
Who lit the spark in the working-girl's heart?

5
Harry Golden's short and square,
Quotes the Bible at the drop of a hat,
Or Charles II or Socrates,
Or Sandburg or Jehoshaphat,
Preaching equal rights for the Blacks and the Whites!

Another friend was coming to Washington. And he had been through an ordeal. I wanted to commemorate his victory and survival:

THE TALE OF JOHNNY FAULK

Let me tell you the tale of Johnny Faulk And the men who tried to give him a
fright, How the black-list boys they se-lec-ted his name And John-ny had to fight for his life!

CHORUS
Did they make him run? No, they did-n't make him run, Though they tried they could-n't scare
John, they called him false names like a red and a trai tor, But John-ny Faulk still fought on.

2
John was sitting with his family in New York City
In the winter of fifty-six,
When he got a phone call from a *New York Times* reporter
That Johnny's name was on the blacklist.

3
It was seven long years till Johnny won his battle;
Louis Nizer stepped up and took the case;
And the jury brought a verdict that restored John's reputation,
And again he joined the human race.

4
Now I think that all you people of this mighty nation
Ought to stop for a minute or two,
And consider the case of Johnny Faulk
And how a blacklist might some day include you!

And I had a good-hearted Southern friend to whom I wanted to give a song. He'd been known to read by candlelight, to assembled dirt-farmers outside of Atlanta, the *Georgics* of Virgil, with which I was familiar, in which good farming techniques are listed, and which begins:

> *What makes the cornfield smile; beneath what star*
> *Maecenas, it is meet to turn the sod*
> *Or marry elm with vine; how tend the steer;*
> *What pains for cattle-keeping, or what proof*
> *Of patient trial serves for thrifty bees;—*
> *Such are my themes . . .*

HE SAYS WHAT HE THINKS

Way down in At-lan-ta lives a man called Mc-Gill, Who writes what he thinks and who thinks what he will.

2

They threaten his family, his life and his home,
But he says what he thinks in the *Constitution*.

3

His eyes have a twinkle, his tongue is his sword,
He's the Southland's defender, and carries its word.

4

There are some name him *Rastus*, some the South's dearest son,
Who says what he thinks in the *Constitution!*

Every day I heard new songs, wondering what would come next.
Some marked news events, many took old themes and tried new ways
of putting them. A few were picked up and others allowed mercifully
to die. I wished that most people in the way that they wrote poetry
for themselves, would also write songs.

I made up silly ones for my offspring; the yellow-haired one, who
was at a university:

SWEET MUSIC

There's gon-na be sweet mu-sic in Wash-ing-ton, Oh, it's gon-na be
gay, When Mis-sy comes to Wash-ing-ton from out Chi-ca-go way!

2

We're gonna get blue eyes and yellow curls,
Black stockings and a skirt that whirls,
When Snick comes to Washington, be a pretty day!

And a version for the red-head, who had got tall and came occasionally to visit, wearing a long sweeping military greatcoat and a
dashing cap:

STRANGE MUSIC

There's gonna be strange music in Connemara,
Excuse me if I sigh,
When John Carl somes a-visiting from V.P.I.!

We're gonna get wild arguments and egghead brains,
All your notions are gonna be changed,
All your values rearranged by a certain guy!

My children were turning their backs on me and taking their separate paths. I celebrated the occurrence in a natural way, in poems. I found I could read her poem easily to the girl; the boy's I put away in my fashion.

AT TWENTY

[*To John Carl Steichen*]

The foreign soil is dusted on your shoes,
You, these many months gone, returned.
The arrogance of conquest is in your stance
As you hurl the door to and enter my domain.
Your fierce voice startles, used to a small son
Soberly erecting erector sets, not even swearing,
Conscientious, religious, within my hearing.
A gentle child! And I employing strong words at times
In a temper, being amazed and thinking you tender
And alien. You were a still boy, who now come
To my room with a loud sound like laughter. Why, I wonder,
Can I scarcely touch your fresh hard face? Stranger!

This evening I glance across to where in a chair
Your cradled guitar makes odd tunes from some land
Where women shield their faces and men go hand in hand
And you tear open black figs large as oranges,
The pink flesh hot and sweet and sensuous.
You have lifted veils; you have with those men
Taken wine resinous, half-warm. There is brine
In your new beard; sinewy your different hand.
In the shadow your mouth glints telling of a dragon
And mermaids, of swine to men and men to swine.
Rocked on my knees in fever were you once mine?
With mouth then like a flower from which now I turn?

You do not know nor ever shall, tall one,
How frequently to my angel I mention
Your name in a bargaining fashion. Let, I pray, this rebel son
Outlive me! no longer any visible part to him.

SOMEONE SHOULD SAY IT
TO YOU, DAUGHTER

[*To Karlen Paula Steichen*]

Someone should say it to you, daughter: love.
Daughter, I loved you when you were three,
The way I loved the golden spaniel pup
Who scampered sunny-tempered on the porch.
You never cried, you laughed;
You never walked, you ran;

You never liked, you loved;
You never spoke, you sang.

Someone should say it to you, daughter: love.
Daughter, I love you best now at nineteen,
The lines of worry there where you have frowned,
Your quiet way of going from a room.
You cry too much, you laugh too much;
You walk too much, and run;
You like too much, you love too much;
You speak too much, and sing.

Yesterday I saw in you no part of me
Although I knew that you were of my blood
And had my smile and had my mother's eyes.
Sister, today you stood before the glass
And took the comb and ran it through your hair,
And looked into your eyes and there saw me
And my mother, and her mother, and hers.
Let someone say it, daughter, sister: love.

I turned to look back into my life; I figured I was about half-way through, and it was time to do this. I gazed upon old days, wondering whether scenes had changed. I was always dreaming of them. Sometimes confused, I would give an old address if there was not time to think, stumbling, "Ah, Harbert, Michigan. Ah, Flat Rock, North Carolina!"

I went down to the bus terminal and boarded one, traveling to the sand-dune country again. It was night when I arrived, and I talked late with old neighbors. But then in the pre-dawn hours, unable to sleep, I got up, dressed, and went over the sand ridge and down to the beach.

There in the light that was still of the night, the dunegrass was orange-tinted. At its roots were clumps of clay-colored rabbit dung, and nearby were dry frost-bit milkweed pods. It was November and the sand was crusted, the moist surface frozen. The wind was not high and the great rollers came steadily. A mist like smoke was coming up from the water. There was the creek of my early childhood where we'd used a great fallen tree stump for a pirates' ship; and its ravine which had been transformed to a world of fantasy. Following the winding ribbon of water, and rolling up from it, was the same dawn steam.

The stars were visible, brilliant as planets, and upon the dune above, in the half-light, was the outline of pines and the clear silhouette of my old home. It was as if affairs were reversed: dream was reality, and reality became a dream. I was entering my dreams.

The light of day approached and a gull swept toward me out of the mist over the water. He lighted up ahead and twenty ghost-gulls suddenly materialized. The bright orange color of the grass was turning into its daytime tawny gold.

There was no one anywhere in the world. I walked in my dream on the sand shelves formed by the beating lake. Pressing my foot on them, half-absent, I watched them crumble. Out on the lake were the pier posts which had once borne lumber wagons, dragged by oxen, loading boats that traveled to the lake ports. They were ruins of an active day. Fifteen posts, indomitable in the steady cruel wash of water, gray-headed. They were the same fifteen that we'd counted as children.

Absorbed in my fantasy, I wandered back toward breakfast, going up the old board walk. Sagged in a hollow beside it were the remains of an ancient cabin. There, wearing rolled paper bags for hats, we had played once, crawling in and out the windows, digging in the deep drifted sand. I shivered in the still November morning.

And then I was on the bus, going home, making a sort of poem, a little angry, a little at peace.

THE VISITOR

Returned this year to the old tall house
Where my childhood was,
Where ever since I've lived my dreams.
Where I've swayed afraid
In a nightmare conceived
Of a long reaching staircase
And wide huge angry rooms of space.
Where a sled drives through softened snow
Repetitively in a place I know,
Where a peaceful fence slopes
And running round a corner my dog speaks.

Wonder if I've laid my dreams
At last, for the old house is
Of its old nobility stripped.
Silent, bare, like a rotted grave-post
It stands. The worst
Is that it's shrunk.
In my mind of childhood I'd made it grow
Larger each year
Like my grandfather's peaches
And cherries, remembered from Luxembourg.
My aunts took him back once
Partly just to stop his stories of the immense
Size of the fruit, to make him see them as they were,
Knotted and tiny and imperfect.

Wonder if it were wise to go,
And to enter square boxed toy rooms
And pass white small unfamiliar doors
Laid out in the same proper pattern. But so
Diminished! Up the short staircases whose walls
Grew in while I was not
There to watch. The falling dust
Smothers old loved cats and dogs
And pet crows that raced
And flew in the sun and gloom
Of my life a short while ago.

172

I was happy to be home again, to my silent flat, to my white and gleaming city. I was looking out of the window as the twilight dropped and the curtains stirred. Neon lights were blinking down the street. The headbeams on the traveling rows of cars bloomed one at a time; their rear red lights glinted. Negro boys went by in shouting groups under my window. I thought of Hughes's line.

> *Night coming tenderly*
> *Black like me . . .*

They were jazzing a tune, combo style:

> *Diamond Joe's a gambler*
> *He must be Satan-sent*
> *He'd rather be a gambler*
> *Than our Vice-President!*
> *Man, oh man . . .*

And then down the street opposite, and rounding the corner, came the whistler that I'd heard so often and looked forward to, in the dawn hours, his notes inimitable, bell-clear, accurate.

It was a song I knew:

FARE THEE WELL

One of these days, with the setting of the sun,
The Lord's going to call this sinner home,
Fare thee well, Oh my honey, fare thee well!

THE END

INDEX OF FIRST LINES

A

Alas, my love, you do me wrong 140
All around the cobbler's bench 127
All around the mulberry bush 9
Amazing grace, how sweet it sounds 124
Am Brunnen vor dem Tore da steht ein Lindenbaum 43
Ara-go-on, you're only fooling 5
As I walked out one cold winters morn 97
As Joseph and Mary were walking on the green 128
A song to thee, fair state of mine, Michigan, my Michigan 40
A Spanish cavalier stood in his retreat 7
As we sailed on the water blue, Whisky Johnny 6
Away in a manger, no crib for His bed 31

B

But black is the color of my true love's hair 140
Bye and bye, bye and bye 11
Bye, baby, bye-lo, what makes you cry so? 5
By thy rivers gently flowing, Illinois, Illinois 39

C

Came a dove through the woodland 16
Carolina, Carolina, heavens blessings attend her 118
Come all you bold sailors that follow the Lakes 52
Come, enter then His gates with praise 126
Connecticut eats the nutmeg, the nutmeg, the nutmeg 118

D

Did you ever ever ever in your leef life loaf? 6
Down at the station 43
Down the Mississippi steamed the Whippoorwill 53
Do you remember Sweet Snick from Connemara? 112
Duncan and his brother was playing pool 72

E

Early on a Monday morning 47
East side, west side, all around the town 151
Elsie from Chelsea 5
Everybody works at our house 78
Every time I come to town 27
Eyes like the morning star 76
Ezekiel saw the wheel 62

F

Flow gently, sweet Afton, among thy green braes 16
Forty-nine bottles, hanging on the wall 64
Frankie and Johnny were lovers 73

G

Go lay the lily low, go lay the lily low 154
Goodbye, I'm on my way 35
Go to sleepy, little baby 4
Great God, I'm feeling bad 77

H

Hand me down my walking cane 130
He went from his palace grand 55
Hold my hand, Lord Jesus 125
How oft I dream of childhood days and tricks we used to play 42

I

I am Jesus' little lamb 30
I don't want to be buried in the storm 119
I dreamed I saw Joe Hill last night alive as you and me 29
I dreamed that I had died and gone to my reward 155
I dream of Jeannie with the light brown hair 141
I dreamt that I dwelt in marble halls 115
If each little kid could have fresh milk each day 138
I found a horseshoe; I found a horseshoe 27
I have got religion, I shall not be moved 49

I left my darling lying there, lying there, lying there 110
I'll give to you an easy chair 99
I'll tell you about a fellow the whole darn country knows 167
I'm a good old rebel and that's just what I am 107
I'm a stranger in your city, my name is Paddy Flynn 23
I'm sad and I'm lonely; my heart it will break 47
In Brooklyn City, there lived a lad 12
In Scarlet Town where I come from 148
In the gloaming, oh my darling 8
It's a short way to Connemara 112
It was down in the valley that's called Tennessee 142
It was one October morning 51
I want to sing you a song about the goat, Jennifer 165
I was a waitress in a Georgia Street hotel 66

J

Jesus Christ and St. Peter went out for a walk 65
Jesus Christ was a man that traveled through the land 81
Jesus loves me, this I know 30
John Brown's body lies a-mouldering in the grave 20
John Carl's wagon got painted blue 114

L

Last night I had the strangest dream 161
Let me tell you the tale of Johnny Faulk 168
Life is like a mountain railroad 96
Life on the ocean wave 51
Like a rose she is fair 82
Long-haired preachers come out every night 28
Lord, build me a cabin in the corner of Glory land 126

M

Mary had a William goat, William goat, William goat 10
Mine eyes have seen the glory of the coming of the Lord 19
My daddy is an engineer, my brother drives a hack 136
My daddy was a miner and I'm a miner's son 154
My heavenly home is bright and fair 96
My sister she works in the laundry 41

N

Nicodemus, the slave, was of African birth 63
"No home, no home," cried an orphan girl 92

O

Oats peas beans and barley grow 14
Oh freedom, oh freedom, oh freedom, Lord for me! 161
Oh, have you been in love, me boys 36
Oh, I belong to a private club 162
Oh, money is the meat in the cocoanut 59
Oh, there was an old codger and he had a wooden leg 127
Oh, they cut down the old pine tree 84
Oh, where have you been, Billy boy, Billy boy? 141
Oh where, oh where has my little dog gone? 18
Oh, you must be a lover of the Lord 65
Old Abe Lincoln came out of the wilderness 150
Old dam Tucker was a fine old man 113
Old dog Tray's ever faithful 35
Old Noah built himself an ark 64
On a Monday morning it began to rain 61
On a summer's day when the waves were rippling 122
On Broadway, in the Bowery, he rambled up and down 152
One morning, one morning, one morning in May 56
One of these days and it won't be long 3, 173
On the first day of Marxmas my comrades gave to me 138

P

Pack up all my care and woe 68
Papa loved Mama 77
Paul and Silas bound in jail, all night long 32
Pris och ära sjuna vi, Herren Jesus som köpt oss fri 145

R

Roaming free as the breeze 108

S

Sam is a man, makes a living best he can 164
Seven long years in state prison 57
She's only a bird in a gilded cage 93
Showers of dollars 66
Sjöman, sluta drömma! 152
Somebody's tall and handsome 55
Star in the east, star in the west 11
Sweethearts or strangers, it makes no difference now 81

T

Take this hammer, carry it to the captain 160
Tell old Bill when he leaves home this morning 45
That seat of science, Athens 71
The farmer in the dell 14
The ink is black, the page is white 159
The man who has plenty of good peanuts 13
Then it's a hoo-raw, and it's a hoo-raw 22
The old west, the old time, the old wind singing through 85
There's a bower of roses by Bendermere stream 70
There's a land beyond the river 158
There's a long long trail a-winding 4
There's a man who comes to our house every single day 67
There's flies on you 30
There's gonna be strange music in Connemara 169
There's gonna be sweet music in Washington 169
The Union is behind us, we shall not be moved 49
The world of tomorrow they tell me will be 150
This land is your land, this land is my land 102
'Twas in the town of Washington 163
Two white horses, two white horses, side by side 34

U

"Under the willow she's laid with care." 157

W

Way down in Atlanta lives a man called McGill 169
Way down upon the Wabash, such land was never known 89
We are a band of brothers and native to the soil 106
We are building a strong union 50
We are climbing Jacob's ladder 50
We fought for the cause of liberty, parlez-vous 15
We live in company houses 60
What a beautiful thought I am thinking 82
What's wrong with the Industrial's average? 166
When cockle shells turn silver bells 146
When other lips and other hearts 91
When the farmer comes to town with his wagon broken down 100
When the union's inspiration through the workers' blood shall run 21
Where did you get that hat? 15
Where, oh where is old Elijah? 26
Wish I was in Tennessee 92
Who's that coming, all dressed in red? 101
Word is from the kitchen and word is from the hall 94

Y

Yonder comes the high sheriff riding after me 24
You can't get to heaven on roller skates 137
You put your right foot in 17
You're as pure as the flowers in springtime 80
You work in a factory all of your life 154

INDEX OF SONGS

A

AMAZING GRACE	124
ARA-GO-ON	5
AWAY IN A MANGER	31

B

BALLAD	112
BALLAD OF SAM YUDKIN	164
BARBY ELLEN	148
BATTLE HYMN OF THE REPUBLIC, THE	19
BENDERMERE STREAM	70
BIGERLOW	51
BILLY BOY	141
BIRD IN A GILDED CAGE	93
BIRTHDAY SONG	167
BLACK AND WHITE	159
BLACK IS THE COLOR	140
BONNIE BLUE FLAG, THE	106
BRADY	72
BRING BACK MY MARKET	166
BYE AND BYE	11
BYE BABY BYE-LO	5

C

CAME A DOVE THROUGH THE WOODLAND	16
CHERRY TREE, THE	128
COLORADO TRAIL, THE	76
COMPANY SONG, THE	60
CONNECTICUT EATS THE NUTMEG	118

D

DEAR EVALINA	82
DID YOU EVER EVER EVER?	6
DUBLIN BAY	35

E

ELSIE	5
EVERY TIME I COME TO TOWN	27
EZEKIEL SAW THE WHEEL	62

F

FARE THEE WELL	3, 173
FARMER COMES TO TOWN, THE	100
FARMER IN THE DELL, THE	14
FLOW GENTLY, SWEET AFTON	16
FORTY-NINE BOTTLES	64
FOUR MARYS, THE	94
FRANKIE AND JOHNNY	73
FREE AMERIKAY	71

G

GEORGIA STREET HOTEL	66
GOLDEN BELLS	158
GOOD OLD NORTH STATE, THE	118
GO LAY THE LILY LOW	154
GO TO SLEEPY	4
GREAT GOD, I'M FEELING BAD	77
GREAT SPECKLED BIRD, THE	82
GREENSLEEVES	140

H

HAND ME DOWN MY WALKING CANE	130
HE WAS THE WORLD TO ME	55
HE SAYS WHAT HE THINKS	169
HOLD MY HAND, LORD JESUS	125
HOSIANA	145

I

I AM JESUS' LITTLE LAMB	30
I COULD NOT FIND MY BABY, OH!	110
I DON'T WANT TO BE BURIED IN THE STORM	119
I DREAMT THAT I DWELT IN MARBLE HALLS	115
I FOUND A HORSESHOE	27
I HAVE GOT RELIGION	49
I'LL GIVE TO YOU	99
ILLINOIS	39
I'M SAD AND I'M LONELY	47
IN THE GLOAMING	8
IT COULD BE A WONDERFUL WORLD	138
IT'S A SHORT WAY	112
I WON'T BE RECONSTRUCTED	107

J

JEANNIE WITH THE LIGHT BROWN HAIR	141
JENNIFER	165
JESUS CHRIST	81
JESUS CHRIST AND ST. PETER	65
JESUS LOVES ME	30
JOE HILL	29
JOHN BROWN'S BODY	20

K

KEVIN BARRY	47

L

LAST NIGHT I HAD THE STRANGEST DREAM	161
LIFE IS LIKE A MOUNTAIN RAILROAD	96
LIFE ON THE OCEAN WAVE	51
LINDENBAUM, DER	43
LORD, BUILD ME A CABIN	126
LOVER OF THE LORD	65

M

MAN WHO COMES AROUND, THE	67
MAN WHO HAS PLENTY OF GOOD PEANUTS, THE	13
MARY HAD A WILLIAM GOAT	10
MICHAEL ROY	12
MICHIGAN, MY MICHIGAN	40
MILL WAS MADE OF MARBLE, THE	155
MONEY	59
MULBERRY BUSH, THE	9
MY SISTER SHE WORKS IN THE LAUNDRY	41

N

NEW YORK I	151
NEW YORK II	152
NICODEMUS	63
NOBODY'S DARLING	80

O

OATS PEAS BEANS AND BARLEY	14
OH FREEDOM!	161
OH WHERE OH WHERE HAS MY LITTLE DOG GONE?	18
OLD CODGER, THE	127
OLD DAM TUCKER	113
OLD DOG TRAY	35
OLD HUNDRED	126
OLD NOAH	64
OLD PINE TREE, THE	84
ON A MONDAY MORNING	61
ONE MORNING IN MAY	56

P

PAPA LOVES MAMA	77
PAUL AND SILAS	32
PHARAOH'S ARMY	101
POP! GOES THE WEASEL	127
PORTLAND COUNTY JAIL	23

R

RED IRON ORE	53
RICH MAN AND THE ORPHAN GIRL, THE	92
ROAMING FREE AS THE BREEZE	108
ROSIE NELL	42

S

SEVEN LONG YEARS	57
SHIP THAT NEVER RETURNED	122
SHOWER OF DOLLARS	66
SJÖMAN	152
SKIP TO MY LOU	114
SOLIDARITY FOREVER	21
SOMEBODY'S TALL AND HANDSOME	55
SPANISH CAVALIER, THE	7
SPANISH JOHNNY	85
STAR IN THE EAST	11
STATE OF ILLINOIS, THE	89
STEAMBOAT BILL	52
STRANGE MUSIC	169
STREETCAR SONG, THE	163
SWEET MUSIC	169

T

TAKE THIS HAMMER	160
TALE OF JOHNNY FAULK, THE	168
TELL OLD BILL	45
TERRIBLY PRIVATE CLUB, A	162
THEN IT'S A HOO-RAW	22
THEN YOU'LL REMEMBER ME	91

THERE'S A LONG LONG TRAIL A-WINDING	4
THIS LAND IS YOUR LAND	102
TOO OLD TO WORK	154
TRAVELING ON	96
TRUE LOVERS FAREWELL, THE	97
TVA SONG, THE	142
TWELVE DAYS OF MARXMAS, THE	139
TWO WHITE HORSES	138

U

UNDER THE WILLOW SHE'S SLEEPING	157

W

WAILIE WAILIE!	146
WANDERING	136
WE ARE BUILDING A STRONG UNION	50
WE ARE CLIMBING JACOB'S LADDER	50
WE SHALL NOT BE MOVED	49
WHERE DID YOU GET THAT HAT?	15
WHERE OH WHERE IS OLD ELIJAH!	26
WHERE THE PRAITIES GROW	36
WHICH SIDE ARE YOU ON?	154
WHISKY JOHNNY	6
WISH I WAS IN TENNESSEE	92
WORLD OF TOMORROW, THE	150

Y

YONDER COMES THE HIGH SHERIFF	24
YOU CAN'T GET TO HEAVEN ON ROLLER SKATES	137
YOU PUT YOUR RIGHT FOOT IN	17
YOU WILL EAT BYE AND BYE	28